DISTRIBUTION

A PRACTICAL GUIDE
TO
PLANNING
AND
OPERATION

BRIAN MARCHANT

**KOGAN
PAGE**

YOURS TO HAVE AND TO HOLD

BUT NOT TO COPY

First published in 1996

Kogan Page Limited
120 Pentonville Road
London N1 9JN

© Brian Marchant, 1996

British Library Cataloguing in Publication Data

A CIP record for this book is available from the British Library.

ISBN 0 7494 1897 4

Typeset by Saxon Graphics Ltd, Derby
Printed and bound in Great Britain by Clays Ltd, St Ives plc

CONTENTS

PREFACE

This book has been written to meet the requirements of those who need a comprehensive survey of the role of distribution in modern business: what its objectives are, how it reaches these goals, how it can be managed as a function.

It sets out to fill the gap which exists between the many books written for the more experienced distribution manager and the knowledge available to the student or manager in another function who needs to have some appreciation of what is involved without necessarily researching in-depth information. Reference will be given to further reading for those who wish to specialise in this subject.

The format followed is that each chapter will start with an outline of its scope and at the conclusion of the chapter there will be boxed highlights containing short summaries. The basic concepts will be explained and then, both by giving practical examples and providing self-examination questions, the reader will be helped to understand how these concepts relate to the real world.

At the end of the text there is a glossary of many of the terms used in distribution which may not be familiar to the general reader.

While this book has been devised to cover, in one volume, the syllabus of the Chartered Institute of Purchasing and Supply Professional Stage option 'Distribution', it should be helpful not only to their students but also to members of the other professional bodies active in this area such as the Institute of Logistics and the British Inventory and Production Control Society. It should also provide a useful reference for those managers who have contact with the distribution process, and need to understand it in principle, without getting too involved in detail.

It is, above all, practical, and the author has tried to eliminate theory as much as possible. In this he has been helped by the comments and contributions of colleagues and students over many years. Special thanks are due to the British International Freight Association, the Chartered Institute of Purchasing and Supply, Chep UK Ltd, Deutsche Bundesbahn, Federal Express, Freight Transport Association Ltd, HM Customs and Excise, Midland Bank plc, RTSI Ltd and Tesco.

Chapter 1

WHAT IS DISTRIBUTION ?

OUTLINE

This chapter considers the basic objectives and structure of distribution. It then looks at the role of information technology (IT) in helping the function to achieve those objectives.

Finally it considers the concepts of trade-offs and total costs, and looks at the question: 'How can distribution add value?'

BASIC OBJECTIVES

Many years ago the author was recruited by a small wholesaling company in the South West of England as commercial manager. Basically the company bought products from manufacturers, stored (and in many cases repackaged) them, and then redistributed them to retail outlets. In the process a gross margin of 17–18 per cent shrank to a net margin of 1 per cent.

Obviously something had to be done to improve profitability. Investigations soon revealed that, although buying margins could be improved, the real area for improvement was in distribution: the cost of storage, repackaging and transport to the customers. Work, which was carried out within two years, took the net margin up to 8 per cent. The techniques successfully applied formed the basis of concepts which were then found to work in other, far larger companies, and which are described in the following chapters.

Developments, particularly in IT and in miniaturisation, have refined and accelerated what can be done, but the basic concepts have not really changed in 30 years. In an often reported quotation Peter Drucker, writing in the US business magazine *Fortune* in 1962, said: 'Physical distribution is today's frontier in business. It is one area where managerial results of great magnitude can be achieved. And it is still largely unexplored territory.'

Some companies – and the superstores Argyle, Asda, Sainsbury and Tesco are good examples – have got this message and prosper accordingly. Others have not and still do not really know the costs of their distribution both in terms of finance and in terms of lost opportunities. As recently as 1995 a study carried out by Andersen Consulting and the Chartered Institute of Purchasing and Supply indicated that more than 50 per cent of large UK companies came into this category.

There are many definitions of distribution. For example, the National Council of Physical Distribution Management (NCPDM) has defined it as:

> The efficient movement of finished product from the end of the production line to the consumer, and in some cases includes the movement of raw materials from the source of supply to the beginning of the production line. These activities include freight transportation, warehousing, material handling, protective packaging, inventory control, plant and warehouse site selection, order processing, marketing, forecasting and customer service.

Whether you completely agree with all of that definition or not, it provides a useful checklist of the activities that distribution and the distribution manager need to get involved with if their role is to be successful.

The core of distribution, in practical terms, is all of those operations involved from the receipt of the request for goods to be shipped from the finished products warehouse to the actual satisfactory receipt of goods by the customer, eg warehousing, packaging and delivery.

The point of business, unless it is deliberately run as a tax loss, is to make a profit. This is achieved by adding value, ie selling an end product for more than the cost of its component parts plus any internal processing (Figure 1.1). The faster goods move through the pipeline (Figure 1.2), the less costs are incurred in storage and transport and the faster the business gets paid. Handling and delay adds costs, not value. Distribution clearly has a vital role to play in attaining a smooth and rapid flow.

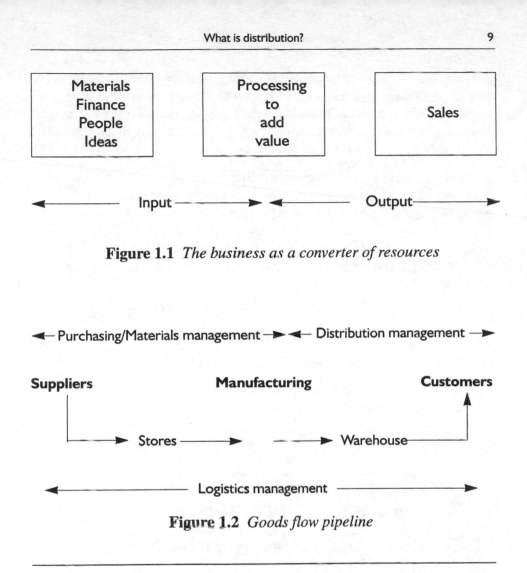

Figure 1.1 *The business as a converter of resources*

Figure 1.2 *Goods flow pipeline*

Self-Examination Question

What are the costs of distribution in your organisation?

The answer to this question will obviously be affected by the business you are in. In a wholesaling company the answer, as a percentage of the total cost, would probably be higher than for a manufacturing company. Almost certainly, however, you will be surprised at their magnitude. J Cooper, in *Logistics and Distribution Planning* (Kogan Page, 1994: 208), states that typically a company spends about 7 per cent of its sales revenue on distribution.

Hopefully you are already starting to think about how these costs, which significantly impact on profit, can be controlled and reduced.

Thinking along these lines then takes us into the realms of structure. In later chapters consideration is given to forms of organisation, but at this stage think about some of the issues:

- centralisation versus decentralisation;
- stand-alone function or reporting into another department;
- in-house or outsourced (to a third party).

There is no one right answer. Structure depends on the type of business involved, the resources available (people, expertise, finance) and often the culture of the company.

Self-Examination Question

What are the distribution problems of:

- a manufacturer of consumer electronics?
- a chain of retail shoe shops?
- a manufacturer of large hydraulic pumps?

How do you think these problems could best be handled?

INFORMATION TECHNOLOGY (IT)

What is the most important part of a juggler's skill – keeping all the balls in the air, or knowing where all the balls are at any given time? Most people, after reflection, would say the latter. (You could always have some of the balls in your hand!)

It could be argued that in management the most important skills are knowing exactly what is going on and then taking the appropriate action.

- How many orders do I have to ship today?
- What is my vehicle availability?
- What is the most effective routeing?
- Do I have priority customers?
- Is there sufficient stock?

These are some of the questions to which distribution must have accurate and timely answers.

The major developments in IT over the last 20 years have made the job that much easier. Human beings still have to take decisions but the information on which these decisions are based can be obtained on line and with, theoretically, 100 per cent accuracy.

Speeding up communication should reduce lead times, and shorter lead times should give better cash flow. The faster goods get to a customer the earlier the supplier should get paid. (In the long run I might even sell him more of my product.)

IT has been defined as:

The application of hardware (machinery) and software (systems and techniques) to methods of processing and presenting data in a meaningful form which helps reduce uncertainty and is of real perceived value in current or future decisions.

The involvement and development of IT is often seen as being a four-stage process. Where a company is positioned in using IT can be the product of many factors, not the least of which is the readiness to accept change in the availability of information both to employees and customers. These various stages are examined in detail later in this book (see Chapters 4, 5 and 10) but at this point in our consideration they can be identified as:

- operational;
- management information;
- adding value;
- running the business.

Operational systems. These perform the basic clerical jobs without the fallibility of human beings any hour of the day or night. Examples in the distribution area would include updating stores records, printing out picking lists, producing transport documents, etc.

Management information systems. These compare actual performance against budget, or some other predetermined measure. By using exception reports they can produce key information in a concise form, highlighting variances. Pareto analysis of stock movements to emphasise the low percentage of item lines which form the bulk of turnover is a classic example, but others could include actual fuel consumption against budgeted consumption, hours worked against estimates, lead times achieved against lead times forecast.

In the instances outlined above IT is not doing anything which could not have been done by human beings; it is just doing it more accurately (providing the data entered is correct), more quickly, and presenting it in a more useful and usable condition. This enables the relevant manager/clerk to take better informed decisions.

Value adding systems. Systems which add value are those which either do tasks which could probably not have taken place before or would have required a considerable increase in staff to achieve them. At the time of writing this chapter trials are now under way of 'Smart' cards which effectively take the place of money. They are loaded with a value – say £100 – and can be used to buy goods up to that value over a period of time. On every occasion that the card is used the value of items purchased is deducted from the value on the card, and the balance is automatically revalued. For example, if I have a £100 card and use it to buy £37 of goods the card is automatically rebalanced to a value of £63 prior to my making the next purchase. At any time, providing I have funds in my bank account, I can transfer more 'money' into my card. This technique, the use of cards which are effectively microprocessors, could well have applications in issuing stores for dispatch to customers.

An existing example of a value adding system, which in many areas is now taken for granted, is the 'spell check' system on a word processor. When drafting a document I can, at amny time, carry out a spell check. The word processor will check every word against its own dictionary and signal any variance between my spelling and the dictionary spelling. It will then ask me what action I want to take, ie accept its version, consider some alternative, or make an override.

Another example is the use of electronic mail. Managers no longer have to be in their own offices to read and deal with mail that has been received in their absence. Providing they have access to a linked terminal anywhere in the world, they can attend to it, irrespective of location or time.

Most of the business journals now have articles on a regular basis explaining how some company has added value to its operation by the intelligent use of IT.

In 1993 *The Financial Times* published an article 'Wired for Trade in Singapore'. Basically the Singapore government has set up an island-wide electronic data interchange network linking together manufacturers, freight forwardmers, traders and government agencies. Delay times of up to three days in obtaining clearance of import and export consignments have been reduced to hours. The reduction in the costs of transport, temporary warehousing, etc, are obviously considerable.

More recently articles have been published detailing the growth of SPIN (Southampton Port Information Service). This uses electronic data interchange (EDI) to pass freight information on to nearly 1000 participants, including ports, airports, freight companies, importers, exporters and freight forwarders.

Running the business. The use of these systems still tends to be restricted to modelling and decision support systems which basically try to answer the 'what if' question. Such systems were defined in 1983 by O Helferich (in the article 'Computers in Manufacturing' in Distribution Management, Auerback Publishers Inc, Pennsaukon, New Jersey, 1983) as 'interactive computer based systems that provide data and analytical models to help decision makers solve unstructured problems – problems with many difficult to define variables'. Where should I locate my new warehouse? Should I buy/lease more vehicles or build more depots? This area is explored in greater detail when strategic factors are considered in Chapter 4.

Self-Examination Question

Where is my organisation positioned in the use of IT? How does this compare with our competitors?

Throughout this book references will be made to or examples given of how IT has revolutionised the application of logistics. Some pundits claim that without IT the barriers that divided stores from transport from customer service would still be there.

MAXIMISING ADDED VALUE

Distribution, like most of the so-called 'service' functions, suffers from being considered as an 'add on' to the real business of buying and selling. Distribution companies exist in their own right, but until comparatively recently few in a manufacturing company saw distribution as a real issue.

A company known to the author was spending £300,000 per month on distribution, and did not even realise this prior to the installation of a new IT system that highlighted carriage charges.

As is so often the case distribution is yet another area where powerful forces could be in conflict. Manufacturing will tend to produce as long a run as possible, finance want to keep stocks (and the ensuing tie-up of working capital) down, and sales will want all orders to be met first time – preferably 'yesterday'. And the customer? Who knows what he or she really wants?

There is therefore a constant search for the most effective trade-off between these sometimes conflicting interests, a trade-off which does not necessarily minimise cost but which will maximise advantages and add value.

By adding value one or more key characteristics are added to the product which are valued by the buyer. This value may be real or merely perceived, but either way it makes the potential buyer want to buy my product, rather than that of my competitors.

This added value can come about in many ways:

- price;
- delivery (short lead time or consistent lead time?);
- quality;
- packaging;
- uniqueness;
- after-sales service.

In several of these areas distribution obviously has a potentially significant contribution to make.

Self-Examination Question

Try to analyse a few of your recent buying decisions.
Why did you really buy Brand A?

In any managerial decision the business is at risk if the desires of the customer are not taken into consideration, and often the customer is prepared to pay a premium for those desires to be met.

A simple example will illustrate this. A wine store regularly delivers to customers in a particular geographical area on Friday. Approaching the Easter weekend, a customer living in that area telephoned an order through and, almost as an afterthought, said 'As this Friday is Good Friday, when will you deliver?' The reply was that no deliveries would be made that week to that area. Result, at least one regular customer lost.

SUMMARY

This chapter introduced three of the major themes running through this book:

- What is distribution and how does it fit into the organisation?
- How can IT help in controlling and improving distribution?
- How might distribution add value?

Distribution is the physical link between the organisation and its customers.

Suggested specialist reading

Cooper, J (ed) (1994) *Logistics and Distribution Planning,* Kogan Page, Chapter 2: 'Assessing the cost of customer service'.

Chapter 2

MOVING GOODS

OUTLINE

In this chapter consideration is given to the physical movement of goods.

It starts by considering the various modes of transport that are available, and their relative advantages and disadvantages. Consideration is then given to the major developments which have taken place, how they arose and what the future might hold.

The chapter then ends by looking at the problems of hazardous goods.

AVAILABLE MODES OF TRANSPORT

Transport may be defined as the conveyance of an object from one place to another. It can take place in any of the three elements known to mankind: land, water or in the air, and it can happen in a physical way (a package on a lorry), or in an 'incorporeal' way (TV transmission). While we have not quite yet got to the *Star Trek* 'Beam me up, Scotty' mode, is it completely far-fetched to think that it might be a method of the future?

At present distribution is faced with six main choices:

- by land:
  — road;
  — rail;
  — canal;
  — pipeline;

- by sea:
  — ship;

- by air:
  — aircraft;

- plus the specialised area of electronics.

Eurasia forms the biggest single land mass in the world (and the greatest potential number of consumers), and with the Channel Tunnel it is possible to drive from the Atlantic coast of the UK to the Pacific coast of Siberia. It is therefore appropriate to commence this survey by thinking about land transport.

The options here are road, rail, canal and pipeline. At this stage note that most transport operations are intermodal. Very rarely do goods spend the entire transit in one medium with one prime mover. At some point or another some crossover occurs, for example out of a ship or barge and onto a lorry, or out of a large transport container and into, possibly, individual parcels.

Self-Examination Question

What are the advantages of moving goods by road?

Road transport. Your answer probably centred very heavily on *flexibility* and *service*. Provided the terrain is drivable, road transport is very flexible and delivery or collection can be made from any number of points without the need for purpose-built terminals.

The requirements of the customer in terms of transport time, guaranteed delivery schedule, etc, can normally be met. With the development of the motorway system most major towns in the UK are within a few hours driving time of each other.

At all times, with the development of two-way radio and mobile telephones the driver and the dispatching or receiving point can be in contact with each other. Security is normally improved because the load is accompanied.

A range of vehicle types and sizes can be provided to meet most requirements from the light van to the 40-tonne (or more) capacity long-distance vehicle.

By its very nature road transport tends to be a private sector activity with intense competition, and there are still a large number of small haulage companies providing both specialist and general services.

The major disadvantages are the increasing impact of environmental legislation, adverse road conditions, and the relatively low bulk that can be carried with the resultant effect on cost.

Environmental considerations are considered in some depth in Chapter 9, but it is appropriate to mention some now. Apart from international and national requirements to reduce lead emissions and regulate the permitted driving hours, axle loading, etc, there are an increasing number of local authority restrictions on the use of roads (the so-called 'city centre' bans), weight restrictions, parking restrictions, etc. In some villages it is impossible for vehicles to deliver legally to those shops which have no rear entrance and which are fronted by double yellow lines! In theory lorries should park some distance away and bring goods in by hand.

Another problem is that of road conditions. With the huge volume of road traffic the effect of repairs to the road surface can cause long delays. Accidents quickly cause major tailbacks, as any regular driver in the UK on the M25 will know. Intemperate weather can also cause a problem.

Nonetheless, a major amount of traffic is carried by road, and it has been argued that any form of 'just-in-time' operation would be unworkable without an efficient road transport system.

Rail transport. In some ways, rail transport is the opposite side of the coin to road transport. Stating the obvious, it needs major infrastructure. Providing there is not too much rain you can run lorries without metalled roads, but you cannot run railways without rails (and sidings). Trains can only run to predetermined points and when the rail head is reached you have to transship.

Rail has the advantage of being able to carry heavy and bulky loads, and companies in businesses such as coal mining, oil distribution and quarrying will use specially assembled trains to move loads from siding to siding at a low cost. Relatively fast transit times can be obtained: a company the author worked for ran 200-tonne shipments of liquid petrochemicals from Scotland to the South of England (450 miles approximately) with a guaranteed transit time of two days (once on the siding they could be unloaded at our convenience).

Railways often offer warehousing facilities which can be used as stock-holding points, particularly where bulk materials are broken down. However, apart from the problems of the supporting infrastructure, there are other disadvantages relating to service and security. Shunting can cause damage and goods need to be adequately protected against impact. They also need to be protected against other goods which, because of their nature, might cause contamination.

Pilferage can also be a problem – in one incident the radios were stolen from a train load of new cars while it was being held in a siding.

Canals. The third major possibility on land is the use of canals. In the UK the commercial use of canals is low but in Europe and the USA barge traffic is still a significant way of moving bulk shipments. Costs are low, but it is not very fast and unless the receiving depot has dock-side facilities, some form of transshipment will be necessary.

Pipelines. Originally for supplying water in irrigation schemes, pipelines have been around for many centuries, but as with so many ideas it took a war to bring about a major change in thinking. In 1944 the Allies introduced PLUTO ('pipe line under the ocean') to transport fuel from the South of England to the advancing armies in Western Europe. This pipeline was basically the sole source of fuel supply until major working port installations were captured.

By 1983 it was calculated that 899 million tonnes of petroleum products per year were carried by pipelines in the USA, while in the UK we have seen the development of the national gas grid. An article in *The Financial Times* by Max Rodenbuck entitled 'Rising European Demand Fills Suez Oil Pipeline' and published on 30 August 1994 reported that 80 million tonnes of crude oil passed through SUMED, the Suez–Mediterranean pipeline. This was double the quantity actually passing through the Suez Canal.

The advantages of pipelines are:

- the ability to move bulk;
- little risk of disruption due to the weather;
- low unit cost;
- low variable cost.

The main disadvantages are:

- high initial cost;
- long transit time (liquids move at about 10 miles per hour).

Transport by sea. This method of transport has some factors in common with the railways. It is good for bulk loads, relatively cheap and quite efficient in the use of people. However, there are the disadvantages of long transit times and the need for an infrastructure of docks and harbour facilities. It is almost inevitable that some transshipment will have to take place at the point of arrival, unless the users have their own facilities (eg, flour mill or large petrochemical plant). Weather can delay shipments, although, providing there is enough sea-room, most vessels can now ride out storms.

As will be made evident later in this chapter, transport by sea has been changed beyond recognition by the introduction of the demountable container and the development of specialised container ships.

Air transport. In many ways air transport personifies the use of the trade-offs. Does speed between air terminals, greater security and the requirement for light packaging offset high cost, size and weight limitations, and possible delays by bad weather? If the goods have a short life, eg flowers, or are required urgently, probably yes.

There is, however, the problem with dedicated freight carrying aircraft of obtaining a return load. For example, cargo companies flying freight from the USA to the UK can have difficulty in filling the plane for the return journey.

The largest air freight carrier, Federal Express, carried 3.2 million tonnes of cargo in 1994, more than three times as much as its nearest competitor (Lufthansa, 909,000 tonnes). Of the top ten carriers four are American.

To develop air transport fully more 'feeder' routes are required and more liberalisation of flying rights.

Electronic transmission. If it can be printed or projected on a screen, it can be moved electronically. Conceptually there is no reason why this book could not be transmitted electronically to any part of the world and then either produced as hard copy or displayed by a cathode ray tube. Conceptually the customer is able to go to his or her local bookshop and get an on-line print of whatever book is required.

In this first section of the chapter consideration has been given to the main methods of transport available. Appendix 1 summarises the main advantages and disadvantages of each method.

Self-Examination Question

What are the macro factors which affect choice?

No business works in a vacuum, and even in the European Union the playing field is not 100 per cent level.

Apart from purely commercial reasons, other influences will impact on the choice of transport medium, particularly when international trade is involved. These influences can be physical or political.

Physical factors range from impenetrable mountain ranges to harbours which are unusable when the wind blows from a particular quarter or roads which may be washed out. There may be quicksands at the otherwise ideal spot to build your rail head or landing strip. Anyone who has ever flown to Hong Kong will be aware of the anxious feeling that the aircraft will not be able to stop before it runs into the apartment blocks!

Political factors include such things as legislation which stipulates which carrier you use, how many employees have to be citizens of that country, where you can actually bring goods into (or out of) the country, what routes you have to follow and even where you purchase your fuel. It is always essential that a check is made of the requirements of the country you propose to deal with or travel through (see Chapters 7 and 8).

MAJOR DEVELOPMENTS

Sometimes it is said that the real breakthrough in transport was not the primitive caveman who invented the wheel but the genius who thought of rounding the corners off. Many of the developments that have taken place, particularly in the last 40 years, with hindsight were obvious but needed somebody to go for the competitive advantage of pioneering the introduction.

Some examples which have changed the economics of the various modes of transport are:

- container ships;
- supertankers;
- wide bodied jets;
- the Transport International Routier (TIR) concept.

Others did not catch on, but might yet still have their day. Cargo carrying airships and submarines had their supporters, and could have worked, particularly with the development of alternative fuels and power systems. Might they still reappear?

Coming back from the realms of speculation, it could be argued that the modern equivalent of our primitive ancestor who rounded off the corners of the wheel was the person who invented the fork lift truck. The growth in use of the fork lift, one of the many legacies of the Second World War, completely changed ideas on the handling of materials, making possible the safe movement of increasingly heavy loads, and the utilisation of vertical storage space. Up till then handling was dominated by how much someone could carry.

The development of mechanical handling equipment and the associated pallet (see also Chapter 6) made possible the development of containerisation which has revolutionised road, rail, sea and air transport.

Once the decision was taken generally to put goods onto pallets to make it easier (and quicker) to handle them, it was a fairly logical system to try to use packages that could be neatly stacked on and secured to the pallet.

Having developed the idea of a uniform palletised load (each pallet carrying the same quantity of product) it made sense:

- to size the pallets so that they made the best use of the load-bearing surface of the vehicle or railway waggon (culminating in the now universal BS2629 pallet);
- to think about how the pallet could be used as the transit medium, hence avoiding repalletising at a later stage. (In distribution a golden rule is do it once and do it right, do not do anything which is not going to add value.)

For many years before the Second World War 'demountable (ie capable of being lifted off by a crane) containers' were used by the railways. These 'containers' could be lifted from the flat bed of a railway waggon and placed on a trailer which could then be moved to the customer by a tractor unit. Every rail siding had its jib crane so that this could be done. The development of this idea, standardised large boxes, which could be loaded and offloaded by a crane onto a ship did not become common commercially until the early 1950s.

However, this development, as already stated, has completely changed the face of transport (see also Chapter 3). Containers are normally strongly built and completely weatherproof. They therefore can be used in all weathers. Built to standard sizes (see Appendix 2) they can be carried on the deck or in the hold of a ship, on a road trailer, or on a railway waggon. Specially dimensioned containers can be used to carry goods in cargo carrying aircraft.

The container, once loaded, can obviously be moved in a number of ways, eliminating repacking when shipments are moved from one form of transport to another. It is quite possible for a container to be loaded in a factory in country A and then transported by rail to the docks where it is loaded onto a ship. The ship discharges at the docks in country B, and the container is put on a lorry for delivery to the customer.

The use of containers obviously offers great benefits to both the shipper and the user. Paramount among these are:

- faster customs clearance at border crossings (see Chapter 7);
- faster clearance at inland depots (see Chapter 7);
- lower insurance costs – less risk of damage, loss and pilferage;
- faster transit times – no delay in repacking;
- greater traceability – each container can be identified;
- lower freight rates.

Paralleling the developments in the use of containers has come the developments in the means of handling them. Specialised container ships and aircraft have already been mentioned, and these are tending to get larger. The Japanese, for example, are now talking of building ships with a carrying capacity of 7000 TEU (20 ft equivalent units each with a capacity of 33.3 cubic metres). Cranes are now available which can handle 50 loaded containers per hour. Ports and inland depots have been built/modified which are completely dedicated to container operation.

As a final thought in considering current developments and the future: Is there a role for unmanned transport? As ship, aircraft, barge and lorry sizes have got bigger, crew sizes have become smaller. Could automated picking in the stores develop into crewless transit mediums, delivering to pre-programmed instructions? Granted it was on a closed loop, but mail was initially moved around the London sorting offices in that way back in the 1930s!

HAZARDOUS GOODS

Hazardous goods are those which either independently, or in conjunction with other items, can be considered to be a risk to health, safety and property. Classic examples would be explosives, flammable liquids, poisons, corrosive liquids and radioactive materials. But there are others, and in the wrong circumstances almost any item can constitute a hazard.

Some years ago a lorry owned by a small haulage company was moving a mixed load of drummed materials from a chemical wholesaler to various customers. The vehicle was involved in a slight accident, but as a result of this two of the containers were ruptured. Together the materials combined to cause instantaneous combustion and an explosion resulted.

Fortunately no one was killed. Who was at fault and could it happen now?

Increasingly we recognise hazards which were previously overlooked or not understood as such. A lot of these hazards relate either to the goods we handle or to the fuels we use, but the hours our employees work and the routes they follow (see also Chapter 9) have also to be considered.

Legislation

There is a considerable amount of both national and international legislation and advisory recommendations covering this area. The best advice to anyone not an expert is to check with somebody who is to find the current position for example with a local chamber of commerce or a freight forwarder.

The basic publication is the *Orange Book* which is revised every two years by the United Nations Committee of Experts on the Transport of Dangerous Goods. This book contains recommendations which, by and large, have been accepted by the major international authorities. These are:

- **by road:** The European Agreement covering International Carriage of Dangerous Goods by Road (*Accord Dangeroux Routier – ADR*);
- **by rail:** Central Office for International Rail Transport covering the International Carriage of Dangerous Goods by Rail (*Réglement International Dangeroux – RID)*;
- **by sea:** International Maritime Dangerous Goods Code *(IMDG)*;
- **by air:** International Civil Aviation Organisation Technical Instructions (often referred to as *ICAO* instructions).

In addition to these international agreements there are specific UK laws. Among the most important of these are:

- The Classification, Packaging and Labelling of Dangerous Substances Regulations 1984;
- Carriage of Dangerous Goods by Road and Rail (Classification, Packaging and Labelling) Regulations 1994;
- The Road Traffic (Carriage of Dangerous Substances in Packages etc) Regulations 1992;
- The Road Traffic (Training of Drivers of Vehicles Carrying Dangerous Goods) Regulations 1992;

- The Dangerous Substances in Harbour Areas Regulations 1987;
- The Merchant Shipping (Dangerous Goods and Marine Pollutants) Regulations 1990;
- Air Navigation (Dangerous Goods) Regulations 1986;

Note should also be made of the HAZARDOUS CHEMICALS Regulations and the TREMCARD scheme.

The carriage of dangerous goods is a complex subject. It can involve specialised driver training, provision of emergency equipment, emergency information on how to deal with spillages etc.

Readers with a practical involvement are advised to contact a specialised source of advice, for example Freight Transport Association, British International Freight Association or their local Chamber of Commerce.

When shipping dangerous goods there is a basic procedure to follow and goods must be accompanied by a Dangerous Goods Note (DGN). These requirements are examined in detail in Chapter 7 (see also Appendix 8).

As is the case with most legislation relating to health and safety there is the guiding principle of the duty of care. The shipper/carrier/supplier must be seen to have acted in a responsible manner.

SUMMARY

This chapter has considered the different modes of transport available to the distributor and looked at the relative advantages and disadvantages of each. It noted that political/nationalistic reasons may have some influence on the choice.

It then looked at the revolution that has been brought about by the development of the use of palletised loads, and more specifically the use of containers.

Finally it considered the problems surrounding the movement of hazardous goods, and gave details of some of the legislation affecting transport.

Suggested specialist reading

Downs, D E (1992) *Understanding the Freight Business,* Micor Freight UK Ltd, pp 101–116.
Freight Transport Association *Year Book of Road Transport Law.*

Chapter 3

MANAGING THE DISTRIBUTION PROCESS

OUTLINE

In this chapter some of the ideas contained in Chapter 2 are now explored in greater detail.

The first section looks at the functions and objectives of distribution management, bringing out the need common to all management processes for timely and accurate information.

In the second section consideration is given to the various ways in which the distribution service can be provided.

Finally a view is taken of the general problem of security in its widest sense – the prevention of loss or damage not only by theft but also by accident. This section includes reference to the problem of returns and returnable packaging.

FUNCTIONS AND OBJECTIVES OF DISTRIBUTION MANAGEMENT

At the beginning of Chapter 1 reference was made to some of the definitions of distribution. By now the reader should be beginning to get some feel for these, and also for some of the opportunities and some of the problems. As with other management processes each new concept, each new piece of information, will expand and develop the understanding which is already in place.

The prime objective of distribution is to get the right product (goods or services) to the right customer, at the right time and place, and at the lowest overall cost.

Attaining this objective involves four main activities:

- customer order placement;
- order processing;
- order preparation;
- order shipment.

Traditionally these were seen as separate activities, often coming under the control of different managers within the organisation.

More commonly they are now recognised as forming part of a continuous process, this recognition being helped by the development of IT, and increasingly this process is coming under the ultimate control of one manager, known as the logistics manager (if the role includes incoming materials) or distribution manager (see Figure 1.2 on p.9).

As far back as 1971 some companies in the petrochemical industry were structured in this way, and it is now becoming increasingly familiar in industry. The supermarkets have, of course, been notably successful exponents of this form of organisation for many years.

Table 3.1 *The distribution chain*

Customer		Supplier		Customer
Phase 1	Phase 2	Phase 3	Phase 4	
Dispatch of purchase order	Receipt of order	Order picking	Shipment to customer	Receipt and payment
	Vetting	Packing		
	Preparation of documentation			
Placement	Processing	Preparation	Shipment	

Table 3.1, developed from that in the CIPS Professional Study Guide *Distribution,* illustrates the process.

As a customer I want my order processed correctly, sent to the right address with the goods or service being of the quality I expect. The transaction should be appropriately packaged and documented, and correctly invoiced. One of my measures of the supplier's efficiency is lead time: how long does it take to complete the activity from the moment the order is placed, and how does this compare with the pre-order forecast?

As the supplier I want satisfied customers who will pay me on time and want to deal with me again, preferably at the expense of my competitors. It is therefore in both parties' interest that the lead time, the time it takes me to fill the order, is reduced. As a customer I cannot use or sell your product until I receive it; as the supplier I will not get paid until you are satisfied – and it is my cash at risk.

Self-Examination Question

How long does it take your organisation to meet a customer's order and what causes the greatest delay?

How can this be improved?

Some years ago the Dutch truck manufacturer DAF discovered that approximately half of their lead time on common items was caused by delays in processing paperwork. How often does 'ex stock' really mean 7–10 days from order placement to receipt?

Order placement

This process starts with the customer dispatching the order and the supplier receiving it. Depending on the method used the delay can range from almost zero to several days (if the order is sent by post and a weekend intervenes). Modern methods of transmission – telephone, fax and electronic mail – enable virtually simultaneous dispatch and receipt. Some companies now permit customers to interrogate computer records (via IT) so that they can check if an item is in stock and then order without referring to a sales clerk. If the order can be received in such a way that it forms part of the order processing activity without modification, so much the better.

The Swedish company Ferro Engres, which has a turnover of SKr 1.8 bn a year, has stated that 90 per cent of their customers' orders are received via IT. Their Director of Logistics and Information systems is quoted as saying 'The vast majority of orders have no human involvement at our end'.

Order processing (also known as sales order processing)

When a customer's order is received it is checked for accuracy, creditworthiness, etc, and transferred into an internal order to release goods. The following points have to be considered:

- Does the customer have an account with the company?
- Are they creditworthy?
- Are their requirements clear?
- Are they correctly priced?
- Are goods available?
- Do I have clear delivery instructions?

At one time the customer's order had to be rewritten on an internal order form and all these details checked manually before anything could happen. Each operation raised the possibility of delay and error. And how often has a buyer chased an order and been asked by the supplier: 'Do you know our reference please, your order number means nothing to me?'

IT obviously has the potential to simplify this area of activity, and some companies have taken advantage of this. Many will have had the experience of the sales clerk reading off the screen while talking. Some companies, particularly in mail order, have so designed the customer order form that effectively the customer is making out documentation for them. By correctly designing the screen on an interactive system the customer does most of the work. All of this helps to improve accuracy and reduce time. And time, as we are so often reminded, is money.

Order preparation

Whether or not customer order processing comes under distribution or some other manager is a matter of organisational choice. The actual picking and packing of goods would now normally be seen as being clearly within the remit of the distribution manager.

A moment's thought makes it clear that order picking represents a significant part of the operating costs of the warehouse (up to 50 per cent), and is another area where trade-offs are constantly being made. Consider some of the aspects involved:

- dedicated storage or random storage;
- picking stock and reserve stock;
- picking staff and replenishment staff;
- stock-outs;
- levels of service.

All of this needs to be carried out in the smallest area possible without causing congestion.

Most organisations (but not all) will now separate goods inwards from goods outwards, and it is a counsel of perfection that you have a smooth flow through the store with no backtracking or double handling. This of course is not always possible. Very few manufacturing companies receive and ship exactly the same quantities and very few companies in general have the same number of suppliers and customers. A chemical company, for example, could receive in bulk from relatively few suppliers, but ship out in 50 kg sacks to a great number of customers all round the world.

- Is all the stock of a particular product held in one place (dedicated storage) or is it placed in whatever spot becomes vacant (random storage)? Random storage takes less space but requires very accurate location recording.
- Is picking stock and reserve stock kept in the same place, or do we have a picking store and a reserve store (beaing in mind the packaging could be different)?
- Are staff expected to do all tasks, or do they pick by day and replenish by night with two separate teams?
- What is policy towards stock-outs and how is this related to levels of service? The last thing anybody wants to do is create a back-order (or is this an acceptable cost? – see Chapter 5).

The answer to all these questions is, of course, it depends. It depends on the business you are in, what standards your competitors set, how you prioritise your working capital.

At the end of the day most organisations measure efficiency in order picking by such parameters as:

- number of picks per hour;
- throughput;
- space utilisation.

Self-Examination Question

How might IT improve the efficiency of order picking?

Packing

Having picked the goods they now have to be prepared for shipment. What form of packaging is required? Again this can range from virtually nothing (a label tied to a can of paint) to something quite complex. What has the customer stipulated? Are there any legal requirements? Is my company trying to project a particular image? What is allowed in the budget?

It has been said that the ideal package is one that gets the goods safely to the customers and then disappears. Certainly environmental problems are increasingly impacting on the materials used, and there are now many regulations and drafts covering the disposal of packaging, and the need to make it reusable.

Do you use one trip packing, or do you use returnable containers? Does the packing have any intrinsic value (using boxes to build huts)? Is it even admissible in the receiving country (a potentially serious problem with some types of timber)?

There are many questions, and trade-offs, to consider.

Order shipment

Shipping the order fills two main purposes: it gets the goods to the customer and it is the trigger which ensures that the supplier gets paid.

It therefore involves not only the physical movement of goods to the correct location, but also the movement of the correct documentation. Some of this, eg a packing note or advice note, will accompany the goods; other documentation, typically the invoice, will be generated by the packing or advice note.

At this stage it is worth thinking through the normal invoice payment procedure. When an invoice is received it is normally matched against the purchase order to check that it has actually been ordered and that the price is correct, and matched against a goods received note (GRN) to ensure that the quantity invoiced is the quantity received. This GRN is often made out from copying the supplier's packing or advice note. It is therefore in the supplier's own interest to make sure that this documentation is made out in such a way that invoice matching is simple and the invoice can be quickly passed for payment.

Some companies want items described in a particular way – and if it is not illegal, why not? They are paying for it. Many years ago a multinational tyre company, presumably in an effort to maintain confidentiality, had code names for all of its purchased materials. If they wanted a load of 'gristic' gristic is what they got (they paid for the privilege of custom-printed drums and the relevant bit of software to amend documentation).

All of the activities discussed in this section can be carried out manually, and at one time were. Many of course lend themselves to some form of IT.

Self-Examination Question

In your own company, or in a company known to you, how many of the activities described in this section are still carried out manually? How could the selective use of IT improve performance?

If a process is capable of being defined with set rules, it can be run as part of a computer program.

PROVIDING THE SERVICE

In the 1960s some of the major companies with a major involvement in distribution started to look at themselves and ask the questions: 'What business am I really in? Am I manufacturing products for sale, which have to be moved to the customer, or do I basically move other companies' products?' Shell were one of the first to do this, and came to the conclusion that a lot of their resources in terms of finance and people were going into the – to them – peripheral business of transport. And so they took the decision to contract it out to a third party. Many companies have since followed their example, freeing capital finance and management time for the core of the business.

In a recent survey quoted in the CIPS publication *Logistics* (September 1994) under the heading 'Choosing a Quality Contractor', author K Roberts indicated that three-quarters of the manufacturers of consumer products in the UK had increased expenditure on third-party delivery services over the last three years.

Any company, irrespective of size, has two important decisions to take:

- Do we provide the service in-house, do we contract it out to a third party or do we have a mixture of both?
- If we do it totally or partially in-house do we buy or hire/lease transport or staff?

Before taking these decisions management have to consider the following.

What is the company's business?

This is the key question: what is being sold, to whom and where are they located? What are the probable developments over the next 3–5 years? When the answers to these questions have been discussed and agreed the responsible manager can start to think through the implications they have for the type of transport to be used, possible location of depots, etc, and from there go on to consider the 'how is the service provided' question.

In-house/third party

Consider first the in-house/third party decision. This is, of course, the classic 'make or buy, make and buy' alternative familiar to most students of purchasing. The same questions and criteria apply.

It is probably sensible to provide this service *in-house* if:

- it is cheaper than using a third party;
- there are no suitable suppliers;

- existing resources can be used;
- it is the only way to ensure control;
- it helps to maintain secrecy.

NB: Some of these reasons could turn out negative in the long run. It is probably more sensible to use a third party if:

- it is cheaper than providing the service in-house;
- it is not worth investing in transport;
- there is no relevant expertise or managerial resource.

Sometimes a combination of two, using both own transport and third parties makes sense, eg using your own vehicles for bulk, and a third party for part loads.

It should, of course, be remembered that at the macro level the in-house/third party decision is a policy matter and should be decided by the board of directors. The repercussions of deciding to contract out the distribution business can be quite major.

Buy/hire/lease

This is the other major decision. Again the normal purchasing arguments apply: Are vehicles, warehouses, handling equipment (and, of course, staff) purchased outright or does the company hire/lease them? The position is complicated by the various tax advantages/disadvantages ruling at a particular time. The manager is therefore advised to check out the position with the company's accountant or finance adviser.

As at 1995 the advantages/disadvantages could, broadly speaking, be summarised as follows:

Buying

- Item becomes company property and can be treated as an asset (if a piece of equipment) in the balance sheet.
- Item can be made specifically to meet company requirements and specifications.
- The company pays for item in full, even although it may not get any profit from it.
- Eventually item will become obsolete/worn out and a replacement will be needed.

Hiring

- Item never becomes company property.
- Item is normally of a standard design.
- Prices and terms are often not negotiable.
- Item is paid for irrespective of usage.

Leasing

- There can be tax advantages.
- There is probably greater flexibility in terms and costs.
- Item could become company property at the end of the lease.
- It may be possible to update the item during the term of the lease.

As mentioned earlier in this chapter, there has been a major growth in leased services, particularly in the last 20 years. These can be summarised in three distinct categories:

Equipment lease

The equipment is leased/hired but operational responsibility remains with the company taking the lease. Typically the agreement will run for the estimated working life, with a possible terminal purchase option. While operational responsibility is with the lessee, the lessor, by agreement, may take responsibility for support services, eg maintenance. The lessor may also undertake to provide a temporary replacement if the equipment is out of service.

Contract lease complete with operators

The lessee provides all services necessary to keep the equipment working/on the road. If delivery schedules are agreed in advance with the management of the company employing the driver *no operator's licence* for vehicles is required by the company using the service. If, on the other hand, the driver is controlled on a day-to-day basis by the company using the service, under UK law they may be required to hold a goods vehicle operating licence, even although they own no vehicles.

Contract distribution

The total contracting out of the service (vehicles, staff, warehouse, etc) to a third party may take place on the customer's premises or at some other location. Very often 'implants' will be provided, ie people who work on the customer's premises and even wear the company's livery, but who are actually employed by the third party.

This is a growing area and an increasing number of companies in the distribution field now offer this service on a long-term contract basis.

A practical example

A company sold its product throughout the UK. Deliveries were made by a fleet of company-owned vehicles direct to customers. Investigation revealed that a large part of the labour cost was incurred by drivers running empty vehicles back to the manufacturing unit. Frequency of delivery ranged from daily in the home area, to once a week in the North of England.

Closer examination indicated that many vehicles were covering the same ground up to a nodal point, eg four part-loaded lorries a week would drive up to Manchester, one would then turn left to Liverpool, another proceed north to Lancaster, the third turn right to Leeds and the fourth deliver in the Manchester area.

A few surveys indicated that if goods could be got to a warehouse south of Manchester, redeliveries could then be made to Liverpool, Lancaster, Leeds and Manchester. A carrier was found who offered such facilities. Solution: one lorry drove to the depot twice a week with a full load and deliveries were made out next day to the customer by the local carrier. Net result: more satisfied customers (two deliveries per week instead of one), less vehicles and drivers required, no overnight stays and much lower costs.

As the business grew more work was subcontracted leaving only the trunking operations to the company's drivers (who, incidentally, were then able to back load with material from the company's suppliers).

Eventually the whole operation was contracted out, leaving a distribution manager with no direct staff, but the responsibility of monitoring and renegotiating the third-party contract.

Premises which the company had been using for warehousing were turned into production areas, the existing vehicles were sold and the whole of the company's capital was put into growing the business.

The company provided a good example of the economic law of competitive advantage – concentrating resources where they gave the greatest return.

SECURITY

At the beginning of this chapter security was defined as prevention of loss and damage not only by theft but also by accident. To feel secure has been defined as 'untroubled by danger or apprehension'. The distribution manager needs to feel secure in relation to at least six groups of people (see Table 3.2).

Table 3.2 *The security interface with the population*

	Risk			
	Theft	*Environment*	*Accident*	*Loss*
Customers	x	x	x	x
Employees	x	x	x	x
Insurers	x	x	x	x
Criminals	x	x	x	x
Shareholders	x	x	x	x
General public		x	x	x

All goods have a value and are subject to criminal activity. This can range from the employee who regards taking the odd item as a perquisite of the job, to the highly organised hijacking of ships in the South China Sea. If goods are stolen the effect is almost completely across the board. The customer, at the very least, suffers a delay, the employee could get injured or killed, the insurer has to meet a claim, the shareholders suffer a reduction in profit.

Environmental risk which has already been touched on earlier and is considered in detail in Chapter 9, affects everybody (remember the guiding principle of a duty of care), while accidents certainly affect those involved and, at the risk of sounding cynical, can diminish the image and hence the competitive advantage of the carrier or supplier.

There are many other aspects for the manager to worry about, including the final category, loss. In the rest of this chapter we concentrate on theft and non-criminal loss.

Theft

As already stated this can range from small pilferage to the hijacking of ocean-going ships. The options for reducing risk will therefore vary with the product, the method of handling and the modes of transport and packaging. One of the claimed side benefits of containerisation was that it reduced pilferage at the docks!

Self-Examination Question

How does your organisation handle the problem of goods security and how could it be improved?

Take advice from insurers, take advice from professional bodies and use common sense.

Loss

Not every item which is shipped out remains with the customer (or even reaches the customer). In distribution these actual or potential losses can be classified under three headings:

- genuine losses;
- returns;
- returnable packaging.

Genuine losses

From time to time a shipment will genuinely go astray. Perhaps the addressing was not correct, perhaps it was left at the wrong point by mistake, perhaps it was overlooked. Whatever the reason a replacement will probably be required, costs will need to be allocated within the shipping organisation, and possibly claims will be made against the insurance company. With good organisation these problems should not happen – but they do, and there must be a recognised system for dealing with them.

Returns

An allied problem in many ways is that of *returns*. For some reason or other the customer wants to return all or part of a consignment. Possibly the goods were damaged and need reworking, perhaps they were not quite what the customer expected. Possibly the customer ordered more than was really required. For whatever reason these are items which have been booked out of the supplier's stock, invoiced to the customer, and now are potentially coming back.

Organisations need to have a policy on how they deal with this, and that policy is probably the result of discussion between marketing, finance and distribution.

The following points must be taken into consideration – and all have cost implications and a security aspect:

- *Carriage of returned goods.* Who pays the customer or the supplier? How is the cost allocated internally?
- *Inspection of returned goods.* Can they be resold or do they need some rework/repackaging first? If so, who pays?
- *Booking back into stock.* An 'asset' (finished product) left the company and has now returned. Unless the decision is taken to scrap it, it will have to be rebooked to stock as it is once more available for sale and should appear on the stock record.
- *Invoicing.* Some action will have to be taken to cancel or amend the invoice issued to the customer.

Depending on the nature of the business, returns can be quite a major factor. In some high technology industries it is not unusual for a piece of equipment to be bought and returned after three/four months (almost a form of hire). In this type of instance values of £x thousand could be involved, so there clearly can be a 'security' problem.

Returnable packaging

The other form of potential loss to be considered is that of *returnable packaging*.

For many years returnable packaging was a headache for all concerned. In theory the supplier charged the customer for the packaging used – cardboard boxes, steel drums, hessian sacks, etc – and passed credit on return of the packaging.

If the supplier got the packaging back (and often it turned up without any form of identification) it was necessary to identify both who it was from, and whether or not it could be reused. Clerks were employed solely to process returned packaging claims as relatively large sums of money were concerned.

As palletisation became general the sums of money involved became even greater. In many companies drivers were given instructions that if they took ten pallets out, they brought ten pallets back. Pallets became highly coveted items and a strong secondary market developed in them.

As is often the case, where there is a problem, some ingenious person or persons will see a market niche for a specialist, and thus the concept of pallet pools developed. From this came the idea of renting pallets, rather than buying them, thus handing the management problem over to a specialised company.

Chep UK Ltd is an example of such a company and the following extract is taken from their brochure on pallet and container pools.

Chep: the pallet pool

In 1975 there were just 60,000 Chep pallets in the pool. Today there are 12 million circulating in the UK and Ireland and over 80 million Chep pallet movements take place each year.

With this many pallets in transit and the cooperation required from thousands of locations and individuals, the pooling system itself could become enormously complicated and yet, in reality, it is quite simple.

- Pallets are hired from the pool on a daily basis.
- The customer either collects from a Chep depot, or the pallets can be delivered.
- The pallets are used to transport the goods and then left, under load, at the point of delivery.

- At this point, there are three options:

  — *either* empty Chep pallets are given in exchange for pallets loaded with finished product;
  — *or* if empty pallets are not required, Chep offers a 'one-way trip' where delivered pallets can be removed from the customer's hiring account, to be collected by Chep;
  — *or* the hire of the pallets can be transferred from one Chep customer to another, helping the continuation of the supply chain.

This element of choice means that Chep is able to offer solutions to suit every customer's specific needs.

(Reproduced by kind permission of Chep UK Ltd, Addlestone, Surrey (tel: 01932 850085), from whom further information can be obtained.)

Many companies still buy their own pallets and containers but increasingly they are rented from an organisation such as Chep UK Ltd, another example of the classic 'make or buy' decision.

SUMMARY

This chapter has examined some of the major components of distribution:

- function and objectives;
- how to provide the service;
- hhe problem of security.

It gives further examples of the continuous need for reliable and up-to-date information, and the constant process of trade-offs in order to attain competitive edge in a cost-effective manner.

Suggested specialist reading

Rushton, A and Oxley, J (1991) *Handbook of Logistics and Distribution Management*, Kogan Page.

Chapter 4

DISTRIBUTION PLANNING

OUTLINE

This chapter considers distribution planning both from a strategic and from an operational viewpoint.

Finally it looks at some of the tools which exist to help the manager.

THE STRATEGY OF DISTRIBUTION PLANNING

Strategy, in a business context, has been defined as deciding upon the major goals of the organisation and the policies to be used to achieve them.

Distribution, as has already been stated, is a pipeline from the producer to the customer. At the beginning and possibly at other points in that pipeline are warehouses and depots; moving goods through the pipeline are people and various modes of transport; servicing and monitoring that pipeline is a network of information systems, most of which probably use some form of IT. Distribution is all about making the best use of those components to secure the customer's business. It cannot be overstressed that the key to a successful distribution system is an intelligent use of trade-offs designed to optimise the use of the resources available.

In the armed forces efficient distribution wins battles (if you are at the sharp end you do not want to run out of ammunition!). In the world of commerce efficient distribution helps to win customers. When asked for the secret of his success the US Confederate General Nathan B Forrest is reported to have said: 'Get there firstest with the mostest.' Not an academic definition but a good one.

The concepts underlying strategic analysis, and hence strategic planning, are the same for distribution as they are for any other activity.

- What is my company objective?
- How can distribution support this?
- What options would achieve this?
- Which is the best?
- Was the objective achieved?

Any management textbook will go into these techniques in great detail, but picking up some points:

- *Company objective.* Is this clear and measurable? 'God make me a good boy' is a pious hope; 'As from tomorrow I will help old ladies to cross the street' is an objective and is *measurable.*
- *Distribution support.* Does distribution strategy support the overall objective or is it at a variance. If the company objective is to give a 100 per cent level of service, a distribution function aiming to run on zero stocks might have some problems.
- *Options.* There is rarely only one way. Have all been examined? Living at one time in Surrey, I had many different routes to my office in Central London (also modes of transport). Most were worthy of quite detailed consideration and had relative advantages.
- *Optimum solution.* Does this give the closest fit to the company objective? What circumstances might cause this to change?
- *Achievement.* Was the objective achieved, and how can this be measured (and is the measure the same as that used in setting the objective)?

Strategic analysis is obviously a continuous process – the world, and our competitors, do not stand still. While not advocating constant change it is salutary to consider that today's solution is often based on yesterday's data. In the words of the saying: 'Experience can mean applying yesterday's solutions to tomorrow's problems.'

At this stage it is recommended that the well-known techniques of comparative advantage and SWOT are used:

Comparative advantage

- What is the company good at?
- What is it better at than competitors?
- Where can resources be best applied? (Always reinforce strengths.)

SWOT analysis
- What are the internal strengths of the company?
- What are the internal weaknesses of the company?
- What external opportunities exist?
- What external threats exist?

Different organisations have varied ways of achieving the best strategy for their business, but will almost certainly include key policy issues such as:

- distribution – in-house, third party or mixed;
- mix of *fixed* locations – warehouses, branch stores, etc – and *mobile* transport – vehicles, rail, air freight;
- deliveries direct to customer or through an intermediary;
- types of transport used – bulk vehicles, small parcels, trailers.

This process is often referred to as *channel selection*. A channel, in the terminology of distribution, is the method and means by which product, and/or its legal ownership, is transferred from the producer to the end consumer (who may or may not be the invoiced customer). Distribution is therefore concerned with two channels:

- the physical distribution channel – the transfer of product from A to B (possibly passing through C, D, E, etc);
- the trading/transaction channel – the transfer of legal ownership.

Distribution clearly has a direct interest in the physical distribution channel and, depending on the roles allocated within the organisation, at least an associated interest in the trading/transaction channel (explored later in this chapter).

The permutation of channels is considerable, as a few moments reflection will demonstrate. For an organisation working in the food-processing industry, the channels will probably be very different from a company making machine tools. For example:

Physical distribution
- Producer direct to customer.
- Producer to customer ex a warehouse.
- Producer to customer via a third-party stockist.

NB: In each case the movement could be made using in-house services or using third parties.

Trading

- Producer to customer.
- Producer to customer (but goods delivered to a third party, eg the customer's customer).
- Producer to financial house to customer (supplying company could be factoring its invoices).

To make the matrix of possibilities even wider, consider a final thought. Often the producer is not the seller. Mail order is a classic example with goods going direct from producer to the seller's customer. If the seller is not adding any material value to the product, why bring it onto his or her premises (see Figure 1.2 on p. 9).

In many industrial companies a considerable amount of equipment is bought in as finished product. If all the seller is going to do is add a name and date and then reship it, why not get the actual manufacturer to do it?

Self-Examination Question

What channels does your company use and how could they be improved?

If the strategy is right, the operational decisions should be that much clearer to take and easier to implement.

OPERATIONAL PLANNING

Operational planning has been defined as defining how resources will be used to help the organisation reach its strategic goals.

In distribution the planner has three main issues to consider, within the guidelines laid down by the strategic plan. These are:

- physical movement;
- monitoring and control;
- documentation.

As a reminder, the aim of distribution is to get goods through the pipeline to the customer as efficiently as possible. Success can be described as the achievement of two satisfactions: satisfaction by the customer (and hopefully more orders), and satisfaction by the shareholders (more profits).

Physical movement

Some studies have indicated that the actual physical movement of goods can account for 25 per cent of distribution costs – a nice juicy target to aim at reducing. These costs can accumulate in many ways:

- double handling (or worse);
- part loaded vehicles;
- vehicles running empty;
- less than optimum route scheduling;
- special deliveries;
- excess fuel costs;
- bad maintenance;
- bad driving.

By sensible planning, combined, of course, with accurate and regular measurement, the manager can attack these costs with some degree of success.

- *Rule 1*. (If possible) go out with the drivers and see what happens.
- *Rule 2*. Who decided the routes, and whose convenience are they intended to serve?
- *Rule 3*. How much time do drivers spend driving, and for how long and why are they sitting in their cabs not moving?
- *Rule 4*. Check out running costs against the industry average.

Appendix 4 gives a checklist. Work through this against your own operation, or one with which you are familiar.

Many software companies now produce vehicle routeing and scheduling packages, and several of these were on display at the International Handling and Storage Exhibition 1995 (National Exhibition Centre, Birmingham, 28 February–3 March). As an illustration, the package produced by RTSI Ltd claims to offer the following benefits:

- savings of up to 15–25 per cent of distribution costs;
- improved customer service;
- reduced route mileage and fleet size;
- honouring tight time–windows;
- maximising vehicle and driver utilisation;
- providing better control of operations.

Sample reports produced by their ROADSHOW system are reproduced in Appendix 4, with their kind permission.

Monitoring and control

The best plans in the world are useless if nothing actually happens to ensure that they are put into operation.

One of the important concepts of planning, indeed of any management activity, is that of closing the loop (see Figure 4.1).

For example, having set up a routeing schedule, information is fed back to indicate actual performance. That actual performance is checked against planned performance and any variances are noted.

Corrective action (if necessary) is then taken to bring performance back to plan. If the variance is outside predetermined tolerances decisions can then be taken as to whether or not the existing plan was too tight or too slack. A revised objective can then be set and the process continues within the new parameters.

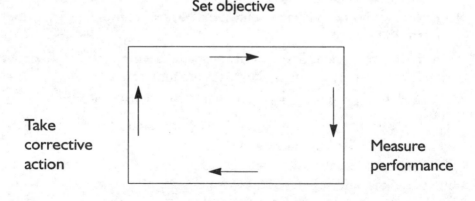

Figure 4.1 *Closing the loop*

It is essential that information comes back as quickly as possible and in this the manager has been helped considerably by the development of tracking and recording aids. At one time, once the vehicle had left the depot, the driver was out of contact until the destination was reached. As part of his job the author, as a young trainee, was expected to know the telephone numbers of transport cafes used by the drivers so that some contact could be maintained. All that has changed, initially with the use of CB radio and now by the major upsurge in the use of mobile telephones.

Not quite such a uniform development has been achieved in the use of vehicle tracking devices, although these are now increasingly in use on public service vehicles, eg fire engines and ambulances. In one version a small transmitter emits a signal which will throw up on a VDU screen the location of a vehicle. The radar displays used by air traffic controllers for years are, of course, an example of a form of vehicle (in this case aircraft) tracking device.

Articles in *The Financial Times* (eg Sheila Jones, 'Car, Guide Me') of 22 August 1995 reported on the work being done, both in developing global positioning satellites (GPS) navigation systems and in medium wave transmitting systems, to fix the position of the mobile unit. It has been estimated that by the millenium 30 per cent of all vehicles in Europe will have a navigation/tracking system and that in Japan it could be as high as 50 per cent.

DOCUMENTATION

In that part of the supply chain which moves goods from the supplier to the customer there are five separate steps in the process which need to be identified to leave a clear audit trail (see Table 4.1). While in many organisations much of the information is recorded by the use of IT, paperwork is still used to a considerable extent, and may be requested by the customer. Never forget, also, that delivery drivers will still need some hard copy, for example to show to the police.

1. *Goods issue note* (often referred to as a *picking note*). This authorises the issue of the item(s) from the warehouse for onward transmission to the customer. This document fills many functions – updating stock records, indicating what happens, etc.
2. *Loading sheet.* This document is another key piece in the informa-

Table 4.1 *Documentation of delivery*

Document	Function	Usage
1. Picking note } Goods issue note	Issuing goods to dispatch	Internal
2. Loading sheet	Identifies vehicle moving goods, goods carried, delivery point	Internal
3. Advice note	Notifies customer of dispatch	Internal
Packing note } Consignment note	Accompanies goods	and external
4. Proof of delivery	Confirms receipt	Internal and external
5. Invoice	Request for payment	Internal and external

tion trail identifying the dispatch point, the vehicle, trailer or container on which the goods are loaded, the name of the carrier, the destination and the date of dispatch.

3. *Advice note.* This document advises the customer that the goods have been dispatched (or, if an ex works transaction, are ready for collection). Another copy (or a packing or consignment note) will accompany the goods. More often than not, the advice note and invoice are generated as part of the same set.*

4. *Proof of delivery.* This document is often a duplicate copy of the loading sheet. When the goods are delivered the driver will obtain a signature from the customer acknowledging receipt.

5. *Invoice.* This document is the request for payment.

*Many of the forms described use common elements of information, especially the advice note and invoice. A majority of companies use

what is called *aligned documentation* in which all documents are produced to the same format, the area not relevant to the particular function
being blanked out. A lot of the forms used in international trade (see
Chapter 7) are produced in this way.

TOOLS TO HELP THE PLANNER

The secret of sound planning is accurate and timely information. In the final
section of this chapter consideration is given to some of the basic tools available. Some have already been mentioned in detail, others will reappear later
in this book.

Basically managers have at their disposal:

- mechanical systems;
- radio/video systems;
- IT;
- bar coding;
- optical character recognition.

Mechanical systems

Tired staff make mistakes and have accidents. Machines do not (or not to
the same degree) and tend to be considerably more powerful. Perusal of
the catalogue of any handling equipment exhibition will indicate the
growing range of equipment now available which basically takes people
out of the equation. If the activity is repetitive and is capable of being
planned the probability is that a machine will be faster, more accurate
and, in the long run, cheaper. The number of picks per employee
attained by the normal supermarket warehouse nowadays would have
been unachievable ten years ago.

In manufacturing industry dispatch tends to be one of the neglected
areas, yet this is the one that gets the goods out – and hence the money in.

Radio/video systems

Reference has already been made to the development of mobile telephones and radios. Another significant advance is the use of radio data

terminal (RDT) systems which allow direct contact between truck-mounted and hand-held terminals with mainframe computer systems.

IT

In most chapters of this book some reference is made to the beneficial use of IT in managing distribution. Providing the data entry is correct and the actual software program is logical, IT is probably one of the most useful tools available.

Bar coding

Manufacturing industry is still lagging behind in the use of bar coding. Bar codes can contain information on product price, storage, users, etc. They can be read by a laser scanner eliminating human translation error, and they are quick. A nonindustrial use of bar coding is the development of the Identichip for animals. A small uniquely coded chip is inserted into the animal, literally in the scruff of its neck. This chip enables all animals to be immediately identified by name, breed, age, name and address of owner, etc.

How many of us watch staff pass goods over the bar code reader at our local supermarket, but still count and identify stock the hard way in our own businesses?

Optical character recognition

Linked with the growth of the bar code is the growth of the reader. Readers fall into two main types, the fixed beam reader (eg pen type readers) which is moved to scan the code, and the line scan reader where the item itself is moved. Equipment has now been developed which will scan at relatively long range.

There is one other tool, not previously mentioned in this section, which the manager should be aware of – the tool of simulation. Simulation – or 'what if' analysis – enables reasonable predictions to be made of the various outcomes. Depending on the complexity of the model, this is derived 'manually' or by a computer-based package. Vehicle routeing, already mentioned, is an example of this approach.

SUMMARY

In this part of the book three important points have been made:

- There must be clarity of the role to be played by distribution in supporting the company objective and the best way of achieving that role.
- At the operational level, within the constraints policy, the best use must be made of the resources entrusted to the activity.
- There must be constant checking and control to ensure that this is an ongoing process.

Reference was made to the aids available to the manager in performing these tasks.

Suggested specialist reading

Christopher, M (1990) *The Strategy of Distribution Management,* Heinemann.

Chapter 5

CONTROLLING INVENTORY

OUTLINE

In this chapter consideration is given to:

- inventory planning systems;
- some basic operational problems;
- using inventory to add value.

INVENTORY PLANNING SYSTEMS

Inventory is both an asset in the accounts of the company, and a locking up of working capital which could well cause serious cash flow problems. It is held to meet the anticipated sales which, hopefully, will materialise.

If there is too much stock going into the pipeline which connects the supplier to the customer, the amount of cash tied up rises; if there is too little, service levels to customers fall, back orders are created and repeat orders may not be placed. Always remember the old saying that you never know the value of the order you didn't get.

Once again there is a trade-off situation. Inventory planning systems try to address this problem and achieve the balancing act of input equalling output.

Like their relatives in manufacturing, distribution systems work basically in one of two ways: either they are responding to a forecast and are therefore, primarily, anticipating a demand, or they are responding to a defined order. Which system is used is again a trade-off depending on the particular mix of distribution channel, type of customer, customer ordering pattern, etc. A supermarket, with an infinite number of end customers but a relatively low number of key suppliers and buying in all of its products will operate in a completely different way from an engineering company utilising small-batch production methods to meet a small number of customers who could well require items virtually made to order. These are very different situations, but both pose an inventory planning problem.

The three main techniques used to control inventory in the distribution channel are distribution requirements planning, distribution resource planning and logistics resource planning.

Distribution requirements planning (DRP1) has been defined as a system which forecasts customer requirements at the point of demand. From these projections time phased requirements for each level in the distribution channel can be defined.

Distribution resource planning (DRP2) picks up the materials flow requirements established using DRP1, and then examines the existing physical resources in the channels, vehicles, warehousing, plant, etc, to ensure that these are matched, modified or enhanced to make certain that the best use is made of facilities.

CIPS students will recognise that distribution is applying the production control techniques of materials requirements planning (MRP1) and manufacturing resource planning (MRP2) to the distribution environment.

In both cases objectives are the same: DRP1 and MRP1 are trying to move away from the static concepts of fixed reorder points, large safety stocks, etc, and match production to demand.

As the perceived scope of IT systems grew, as MRP1 and MRP2, DRP1 and DRP2 were seen to bring real cost and efficiency benefits into organisations, and as the concept of the supply chain developed, growing impetus was given to the thought that, perhaps, the total flow from supplier to customer should be coordinated. Back in the 1980s a colleague told the author that he couldn't possibly plan the production of a TV set factory if he didn't know (a) what the sales order book was and (b) who (the retailers) held stocks of finished product.

From these and similar activities and thoughts came the development of logistics resource planning (LRP) combining manufacturing and distribution resource planning systems (MRP2 and DRP2) in an integrated manner. This gives total control of the entire logistics system from supplier to customer.

As can be seen from Figure 5.1 distribution planning systems cannot stand alone. There must be interfaces both inside and outside the organisation.

Materials requirements	Distribution requirements
Production planning	Sales planning
Capacity planning	Shipping
	Capacity planning
Manufacturing resource planning	Distribution resource planning

| Logistics | resource | planning |

Figure 5.1 *The planning matrix*

The internal contact points should be clear to the manager. There must be linkage between production, in its broadest sense, sales and distribution. That linkage *must* be via a common database so that like is always compared with like. There must not be different forecasts used in various parts of the organisation. Finally, care must be taken to eliminate the lie/mistrust factor. The author carried out some research a few years ago into why a particular company carried excess stock. The basic answer was that sales management didn't believe production would meet the programmes and deliberately quoted too high quantities and too short lead times. Production didn't believe sales knew what they were talking about and deliberately made more than required in a shorter time span. Net result 20 per cent too much stock. In case this is thought to be an isolated instance the same phenomenon has been noticed in other companies with separate planning organisations for production and sales.

Self-Examination Question

What are the planning interfaces in your organisation?
How could they be improved?

The answer to this question obviously will relate to the business. It would probably cover some or all of the following:

- manufacturing:
  - MRP1 and 2;
  - finished goods;
  - work in progress;
- sales/marketing
  - sales forecast;
  - sales order processing (SOP);*
  - electronic point of sale (EPOS).

*In some companies SOP is considered part of the distribution process (see Chapter 3).

To end this section consider the external interfaces between the organisation and its suppliers and customers. Do the systems interface? A significant number of companies now investigate prospective suppliers' planning systems before they do business. If a partnership sourcing relationship is envisaged some direct communication between systems may be essential.

BASIC OPERATIONAL PROBLEMS

In considering the basic problems facing inventory control it helps to start by stepping back and thinking through why suppliers and their customers actually do hold stock. Primarily it is the result of a lack of confidence because:

- suppliers don't believe the customer knows what he or she wants and why;
- customers don't believe that suppliers (including their manufacturing colleagues) will produce what they say they are going to produce, to the agreed quality, on the agreed days;
- either party does not completely believe in their own ability to do their job correctly.

Stock is an insurance, a cushion (hopefully) against things that might go wrong. Like all insurances there is a premium. The premium is not only the money tied up in stock, but also the cost of the space it occupies, the cost of security, the risk of deterioration, the cost of double handling, etc.

At the back of any stock-holding decision is a forecast. The supplier forecasts sales and the customer forecasts demand. These forecasts probably allow for variables, eg major sales promotion, changes in the weather pattern, but cannot cater for the unknown, for example the so-called 'Act of God', or unforeseen action by government. They can also be thrown by sudden changes in fashion, or by unanticipated action by a competitor.

There are many ways in which the forecast could have been made ranging from the wet finger in the air approach of born entrepreneurs to the mathematically precise projection of past demand, cross referenced by almost every variable ever known. The important thing to remember, of course, is that a forecast is a guess; it may be a good guess, it may be a bad guess but it is still only an opinion. So often organisations blindly follow the forecast even though it is obvious that, for whatever reason, it is not being met. There must be a closed loop mechanism to ensure that reality is fed back to tune the forecast to a nearer approximation of what is actually happening.

In a typical distribution chain there will be several opportunities for building in these feedback loops. There must also be facilities for the inevitable corrective action to be taken quickly and efficiently.

Not necessarily in order of priority, decisions have to be taken in the following areas:

- stocking points;
- general parameters;
- allocation rules;
- replenishment rules.

Stocking points

What is going to be stocked where, and how much? Does distribution operate from one store, or from sub-stores in different geographical areas? Every time goods are taken off a vehicle, stored and then reloaded costs are incurred. Once again there is a trade-off situation. *Maister's Law* (also known as the square root law) states that the total inventory needed within a system is proportional to the number of locations at which the product is stocked. The lower the number of stocking points, the lower the overall level of stock. The formula and an example are given in Figure 5.2.

$$1-\left[\frac{\sqrt{x}}{\sqrt{y}}\right]$$

where x = proposed number of depots;
               y = current number of depots.

If there are currently nine depots and it is proposed to reduce them to four, the theoretical stock reduction would equal to:

$$1-\left[\frac{\sqrt{4}}{\sqrt{9}}\right]$$

$$=1-\frac{2}{3}$$

$$= 33.3 \text{ per cent, ie one third}$$

Figure 5.2 *The formula for Maister's Law*

General parameters

No company works in a vacuum and any company ignores the wishes of its customers and the pressures of competition at its peril. Business, it has been said, would be comfortable if it wasn't for the outside influences, suppliers, customers and government who are continually spoiling the best laid plans.

These influences have to be in the forefront of the manager's mind in planning the system.

- What level of service do my customers require (and my competitors provide)?
- How volatile is the market?
- How is the market structured?
- What is the ordering pattern?

Different markets are set up in different ways, and customers have, at the minimum, the expectations of that market. What, for example, would be considered as perfectly acceptable practice if the company were distributing builders' sundries would not be acceptable to the food industry, with the problems of shelf life, cosmetic appeal, special promotions, etc.

Allocation rules

From time to time goods will be in short supply. Is there a policy for dealing with such a situation, or is it up to individual managers to take their own decisions?

Self-Examination Question

How does your company, or a company known to you, handle this problem? Could it be improved?

The nature of the business will affect the answer – but there are all sorts of possibilities. Some realistic alternatives could be:

- give priority to customers who pay you on time;
- first come, first served;
- rationing (everyone gets 20 per cent of their order);
- fill all the orders that do not create remains (ie if we have 20 units available and orders for 3, 1, 2, 6, 4, 7 and 9 units, ship the orders for 1, 2, 4, 6 and 7);
- favour biggest customers;
- favour new customers.

Obviously the decision is not just the prerogative of distribution; sales/marketing will clearly have an opinion.

Replenishment rules

How are stocks replenished at local level? Is the trigger point an order level – every time the stock falls to ten, reorder; or is it time based – the first Tuesday in each month review the stock of rubber boots?

It could even be a combination of both, particularly if the item is seasonal. If, for example, the company is distributing waterproof clothing in the UK, it is not unreasonable to assume that, unless there are any promotions running, the bulk of deliveries will be required during late autumn/early winter. In these circumstances reordering could be carried out on a time-based review in August–February, reverting to an order level review in March–July.

Is the product a stand-alone item, or does it fit into a range? If I sell shoes I know my best sellers in men's styles will be UK sizes 8/10; I would, however, be foolish not to keep some smaller and some larger sizes – particularly if I have major customers who will buy across the range. If that customer is buying protective clothing for issue to staff, a part-delivered order will not help industrial relations.

Added value

How can stock add value?

Before answering this question it is probably helpful to look at the definitions of types of stock given by Coyle, Bardi and Langley in *The Management of Business Logistics* (West, 1992). Their view was that, from a marketing viewpoint, there were seven different types of stock:

1. *Cycle stock:* stock held to respond to demand or usage that will occur under normal conditions of demand and lead time.
2. *In transit stock:* stock dispatched but not yet received by the customer and not yet paid for (NB imprest stock and consignment stock).
3. *Safety stock:* stock held to act as a buffer against unexpected fluctuations in demand.
4. *Seasonal stock:* stock produced throughout the year for a short seasonal selling period. (Good examples are Easter eggs and Christmas trees.)
5. *Promotional stock:* stock accumulated to service a particular sales drive or promotion.
6. *Speculating stock:* stock accumulated in anticipation of a price increase or supply constraint (which might be artificial).
7. *Dead stock:* products which no longer sell in their normal market.

All of these types of stock, if properly managed, can be used to create a competitive advantage, making the potential customer want to buy your product. (Yes – even dead stock.)

Self-Examination Question

Look again at the categories of stock. How could they add value to your organisation?

In some cases the answers are fairly obvious, but others might not be so apparent.

Consider the use of imprest and consignment stock. There is a cost to the supplier in that the value of the material is on his charge until the customer draws it out. On the other hand, delivery costs will probably be lower (one bulk shipment instead of many small deliveries), and the customer is locked into the supplier. Because the stock is physically available there is less risk of stock- outs, emergency orders, etc – all of which generate cost. Finally it can provide a good bridge to other business.

Dead stock might seem to be a peculiar candidate for adding value. There could, however, be a market for it away from the normal channels, giving the opportunity for business which does not damage existing customers. For example, Douglas DC 3 aircraft, first designed in the 1930s, are still flying on small feeder airlines and require spares. An item which is no longer fashionable in the western world could well have a market elsewhere.

Just in time

Any consideration of using stock to add value cannot end without some exploration of the just in time (JIT) philosophy. Most companies would probably agree that the ideal is no stock, supply is matched to demand, and the pipeline is always flowing. Unfortunately the world is not like that, although advances in IT making it possible to reduce transit times – both of material and information – have brought it a little nearer. The JIT philosophy is that goods and materials are delivered exactly where and when required, literally just in time for them to make the next move along the supply chain. Ideally a supermarket requires goods to arrive just in time to support sales.

The benefits of this can be considerable:

- Most of the stock can be devoted to core objectives (selling goods not storing them).
- Many shelf life problems will disappear.
- Much double handling (vehicle to store, store to sale area/work place) will be eliminated.
- Cash flow requirements could be reduced (particularly if customers pay on an 'as purchased' basis).
- Working capital tied up (and possible interest charges) will diminish.

If, as a supplier, I can guarantee my customer this facility, I have a clear competitive advantage over other companies. In some activities such as the multiple retail trade, the consumer electronics industry and the motor industry, a JIT facility must be offered even to get on to the tender list.

JIT does not happen overnight, nor does the concept of partnership sourcing/co-managership which often accompanies it. A colleague of the author once said: 'It is like a successful marriage it takes time, you must have common key interests, you have got to work at it, and from the start you both envisage a continued relationship.' For JIT to work:

- the business has to be important to both of you;

- suppliers and customers must be in close travelling proximity;

- demand must be regular;

- communications must be timely and efficient;

- there must be time to establish mutual trust.

SUMMARY

In this chapter we have looked at the ways in which inventory can be controlled and the problems which have to be thought through to achieve that control.

The chapter ended by looking at some of the ways in which inventory could be used as a means of winning business.

Suggested specialist reading

Rushton, A and Oxley, J (1991) *Handbook of Logistics and Distribution Management,* Kogan Page.

Coyle, JC Bardi, EJ and Langley Jr, C John (1992) *The Management of Business Logistics,* West Publishing Co.

Chapter 6

INTERNAL DISTRIBUTION

OUTLINE

Internal distribution involves fixed assets, mainly warehouses and buildings, and variable assets, equipment and people.

In this chapter we look at both and the way in which one often interacts with the other, again producing the classic trade-off situation.

Throughout the process we are trying to eliminate bottlenecks, double handling, waiting time and anything which adversely affects the cost efficiency of the operation.

FIXED ASSETS

The ideal warehouse has a flat floor capable of bearing any load and a high ceiling with a roof that does not require supporting pillars, giving unrestricted floor space. It will be situated with easy access to motorways and possibly the railway, with no domestic housing within several miles radius. Suppliers will deliver at one end and dispatches will be made at the other and there will be plenty of parking and vehicle marshalling space. It will not be subject to any extremes of wind or temperature and, preferably, will not cost anything.

If that sounds like a daydream, look at the out-of-town facilities being built now, as compared with the buildings used even 30 years ago.

A major feature of the distribution business has been the development of large warehousing complexes within easy reach of major motorway networks. Tesco, for example, now service the whole of the South West from one huge depot close to a major motorway junction (M4/M5).

Tamworth, in the West Midlands, is now one of the fastest growing distribution centres in the country, claiming that 80 per cent of the UK population is within four hours driving distance. Again there is close proximity to motorways, in this case the M6/M42 network.

There are therefore two big policy questions to be considered:

1. What type of warehouse?
2. Where (and how many)?

What type of warehouse will depend to some extent on the business (and the finance available). Appendix 5 gives a checklist which should be helpful in making such decisions.

Where (and how many) is probably more judgemental. National planners have been known to change the route of motorways and bypasses. Techniques range from the simple 'grid and string' method (also known as the tonne/centre method) to complex software programs.

All are trying to establish the ideal location which will give the lowest tonne/kilometre cost of goods movement. They involve a calculation or simulation of the effect of the traffic generated to the various delivery points, and hence the most logical place for the warehouse to be placed. Maister's law should always be kept in mind – the greater the number of warehouses the larger the stocks. Remember also the alternatives of owning the facility or renting/leasing the facility (and the associated services).

VARIABLE ASSETS

Variable assets, in this context, are the equipment we buy or hire to operate the warehouse. Primarily we are looking at things that contain stock and enable us to make the best use of available space – racking, pallets, bunkers, etc – and things that move stock – cranes, fork lift and pallet trucks, conveyors and lifts.

Any reputable supplier of storage or handling equipment will let you have a brochure showing their wares, and any of the major trade journals or exhibition catalogues will contain pages of advertisements. However, in this section we shall consider some of the major alternatives in some detail.

Racking

Racks can be obtained in all shapes and sizes, ranging from conventional racking designed to take pallets to complicated structures designed to take specialised equipment. Racks are normally, but not always, fixed in their location. Their size and carrying capacity obviously depends on features like the loading that can be taken by the floor, the amount of height available, and the capacity and mobility of moving equipment.

Mobile storage

This can take two forms: either *mobile binning* or *carousel* systems. Mobile binning works on the principle that instead of the racks or bins being fixed they are on tracks so that they can be moved either manually or by small motors. The racks/bins can be placed close to each other, leaving one rack width in each row vacant. This means that access can be obtained to any row without the necessity for individual gangways. (In Fig 6.1(b) Bin 2 in row C has been moved to the right to give access to Bin 2B.)

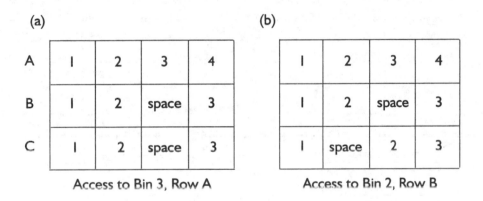

(a)   (b)

Access to Bin 3, Row A   Access to Bin 2, Row B

Figure 6.1 *Mobile storage*

A carousel system is also a method of making better use of space. The bins or storage trays are located in a rotating device, so that the bin to be worked on can be brought to the level of the operator. Good examples of a carousel system are the rotating display stands to be found in bookshops carrying paperbacks and the self-dispense units found in snack bars.

Pallets have been mentioned in a previous chapter. They range from the simple flat platform to box and post pallets which can have sides and posts (either fixed or detachable) to permit superimposed stacking. In addition to fixed locations for storing bulk materials – bunkers, silos, etc many manufacturers now produce mobile containers which combine capacity with manoeuvrability. Again reference to any storage equipment catalogue will indicate the great range of equipment available, which enables you to follow the maxim – *think cubic.*

Moving goods

Methods of moving goods from location to location are also many and varied. Options to be considered include fork lift trucks, fixed or mobile cranes, fixed or mobile conveyors and goods lifts. They can range from the manufacturers' standard items to a product designed specifically for a particular activity.

In theory, there are clearly a great number of options to be considered, before any firm decision is taken as to the configuration of the warehouse(s), and the equipment and staff needed to operate it.

There are also a great number of criteria which have to be established in order to set up the policy framework against which options can be evaluated. These criteria cover general points, as well as the specific issues of warehouse operation and manning.

Self-Examination Question

How would the warehousing requirements of a company distributing domestic electrical appliances (refrigerators, freezers, etc) differ from those of a company distributing rubber boots?

Appendix 6 gives a general checklist of vital points to think about when considering warehouse facilities.

SUMMARY

- Make the best use of space.
- Do not double handle if you can avoid it.
- Think first.
- The distribution warehouse is the door to the outside world of customers. Make yours as accessible as possible. Do not become the business prevention department.

Suggested specialist reading

Jessop, D and Morrison, A (1994) *Storage and Supply of Materials,* Pitman.

Chapter 7

DISTRIBUTION OUTSIDE THE EUROPEAN UNION

OUTLINE

This chapter gives an overview of the major problems which confront the exporter of goods and in particular the requirements of documentation, finance and transport.

It then considers the major export controls and the way in which they operate, and the role of Customs and Excise.

Finally it looks at some of the international bodies which regulate or promote trade including the World Trade Organisation and the International Chamber of Commerce.

THE PROBLEMS OF EXPORTING GOODS – COMMERCIAL DOCUMENTATION

Whoever it was who said, many years ago, that 'exporting is fun' either had a masochistic sense of humour or had never done the job. When we buy, or sell, goods within our own country there are all sorts of activities which take place, often without any conscious action on our part. By and large, goods are bought, delivered and paid for, without any great thought being given to the mechanisms which cause this to happen.

In international transactions, even within the European Union (EU), this is not the case. Both the buyer and the seller need to remember at all times that there are four basic contracts which have to be implemented and controlled. These are:

● contract of sale or purchase;
● contract of freight;

- contract of finance;
- contract of insurance.

Helping or hindering the parties to the agreements will be the various national and international bodies who provide the framework within which business is carried out. Distribution, as the mover of goods, has a major responsibility to ensure that it all happens, and that the various requirements are met.

Distribution may or may not be involved in the negotiation of the sales or purchase contract. They certainly have a general interest in whose law governs the contract and what, if any, are the provisions for arbitration. And they have a specific interest in:

- terms of carriage including insurance;
- method of carriage;
- points of delivery;
- supporting commercial documentation;
  — bills of lading (freight);
  — certificate of insurance;
  — commercial invoice ⎫
                         ⎬ (finance);
  — letter of credit   ⎭
  — documentation required by Customs and Excise.

In an international contract goods are going from company A, based in one country, to company B, based in another country. These countries could be thousands of miles apart with different language, laws, cultures and standards. While getting from seller to buyer the goods may well cross the boundaries and air space of other states which have no specific interest in the deal, apart from protecting their own position.

The contracts, and their supporting documentation, have to reflect this, so that all parties are aware of their rights and responsibilities.

Terms of carriage including insurance

INCOTERMS 1990 define the responsibilities of buyer and seller. Published in both English and French by the International Chamber of Commerce (ICC) INCOTERMS are used throughout the world.

Although not mandatory, by using them both parties to a contract reduce the risk of misunderstanding and possible legal dispute. They cover all aspects of the movement of goods including freight costs, insurance, responsibility for paying dock dues, responsibility for paying customs duties, etc. They fall into four groups:

Group E (Departure)	EXW	Ex works
Group F (Main carriage unpaid)	FCA	Free carrier
	FAS	Free alongside ship
	FOB	Free on board
Group C (Main carriage paid)	CFR	Cost and freight
	CIF	Cost, insurance and freight
	CPT	Carriage paid to
	CIP	Carriage and insurance paid to
Group D (Arrival)	DAF	Delivered at frontier
	DES	Delivered ex ship
	DEQ	Delivered ex quay
	DDU	Delivered duty unpaid
	DDP	Delivered duty paid

Supporting commercial documentation

The main commercial documents normally required are:

- bills of lading;
- certificate of insurance;
- commercial invoice;
- letter of credit.

Samples of these documents appear in Appendix 6 (courtesy of HSBC Trade Services).

Bill of lading

The bill of lading (B/L) has been defined as the receipt given to the exporter by the shipping company for goods accepted for transport by sea. When in negotiable form it conveys the title to the goods.

There are many types of bills of lading to cover particular circumstances – through bills (when more than one carrier has to be used), combined transport (when multi-modal transport is going to be used), groupage bills, transshipment bills and container bills. The important point to remember is that, irrespective of the type and form of the bill, they can all be grouped under three important categories:

- clean;
- dirty;
- stale.

A *clean* bill of lading is one that has not been endorsed in any way. It therefore signifies that when the consignment was shipped there were no shortages or damage and the packaging was satisfactory. A *dirty* bill of lading is one that has been endorsed for some reason. This would normally be because of shortage or damage. A *stale* bill of lading is one when the bill of lading arrives after the goods. For reasons which will become clear when payment mechanisms are discussed, a clean bill of lading is desirable.

Although the vast majority of international trade is carried out by sea, considerable movements take place by air or surface transport. However, an *airway bill* or a *CIM consignment note* (rail), while giving evidence of goods and their apparent condition, is *not* a document of title.

Certificate of insurance
As its name implies this gives proof that the goods are covered for damage or loss during transit. The normal rule of thumb is to insure for 110 per cent of the value.

Commercial invoice
The commercial invoice is the claim for payment for the contracted goods. It is the basic document used by customs authorities in assessing duty and freedom of entry, and is therefore often 'legalised' by either a chamber of commerce or the appropriate consulate.

Letter of credit
A letter of credit (LOC) is a written undertaking from a bank that it will pay the beneficiary (the exporter) so long as he or she meets the conditions of the credit. It interposes between the buyer and the seller a third party who will only process payment when documentary evidence has been produced (eg a clean bill of lading) to indicate that required actions have taken place.

There are two types of credit:

- *revocable* – can be cancelled or amended at any time, by either party. It is therefore seldom used;
- *irrevocable* – cannot be cancelled without the agreement of both parties. It therefore gives the exporter the guarantee that, if the agreed terms are met payment will be made.

The most common forms of LOC are:

- confirmed;
- unconfirmed;
- transferable;
- revolving.

A confirmed irrevocable LOC is one where the confirming (local) bank undertakes to make payment to the exporter if the overseas bank defaults. If the LOC is unconfirmed there is no such undertaking. A confirmed irrevocable LOC is therefore 'belt and braces' as far as the exporter is concerned.

A transferable LOC is one where the exporter can transfer the benefit to a third party, eg his or her own supplier. So company A (the exporter) could sell to company B (the importer) but transfer the payment to company C (A's supplier).

A revolving LOC is a form of 'imprest' credit, often used when a number of shipments are made at intervals. A credit is established for a defined value and quantity with the provision that once a shipment has been made and paid for, the credit is automatically renewed, thus permitting the next shipment.

LOCs get round the problem of two parties who may not know each other and have conflicting interests doing business. The buyer does not want to pay until the goods have been received, the seller wants to be paid as quickly as possible. The bank only releases money when it receives documentary evidence that the goods have been shipped, or made available for shipment, depending on the terms of the contract.

The banks, naturally, make a charge for this service. They also need to be satisfied that everything is in order before making payment. LOCs have not been paid because of relatively minor discrepancies in documentation. The Institute of Export reported in 1994 that at least half of all LOCs have to be amended before payment can be made. The experience of the Manchester office of a major bank in 1993 was that 65 per cent of LOCs and accompanying documents presented to them were discrepant. In one case an LOC was not honoured because of a spelling mistake on one word which was spelled correctly in other documents. Remember, any query means, at the least, a delay in payment. Distribution must ensure that all of the documents required tell the same story, and agree in all details.

If a relationship is established exporter and importer may well move into 'open account' methods of settling charges – money transfer by direct payment from bank accounts – but a considerable amount of business is done, and will continue to be done, by LOC.

EXPORT CONTROLS: THE ROLE OF CUSTOMS AND EXCISE

In theory all goods entering or leaving a country, or merely passing through, are subject to control and payment of duty. The Customs and Excise department(s) of the country(ies) concerned are responsible for exercising that control and collection.

The duties of Customs and Excise cover three main areas:

- the surveillance and prevention of movement of prohibited goods;
- collecting payment of duty on all goods;
- the compilation of trade statistics.

In the UK HM Customs and Excise are also responsible for the administration and collection of most of the indirect taxes levied, specifically VAT (see also Chapter 8 on VAT).

The control of prohibited goods

Import and export controls can be established for many reasons, mainly political or economic. They may be temporary or of a more permanent nature and because many are created for political reasons the exporter or importer must keep up to date on the current situation. Countries which are not well regarded at the moment could well be seen in a different light in six months time, with a resulting change in controls.

Controls normally exist for the following reasons:

- preserving national security/political considerations;
- protecting the public;
- protecting selected industries;
- protecting the currency.

They may be imposed unilaterally (eg by the UK) or by an international group (eg by the EU) or by a world organisation (eg under GATT).

National security/political considerations

One of the most well known examples of recent years was the 'gun parts to Iraq' episode. Another illustration was the restrictions placed on the supply of various items (including electric light bulbs) to countries which originally formed part of Yugoslavia. Normally, however, these restricted items are high-technology based. During the Cold War period very severe restrictions were imposed by the USA. There was a long list of countries (mostly Eastern bloc) to which goods could not be exported directly or indirectly from the USA, either in their original form, or incorporated in some other product, without the express permission of the US government.

Protecting the public

This can range from harmful substances to counterfeit or pirated goods.

Dangerous substances must be accompanied by a dangerous goods note (DGN) and the procedures set out in Appendix 8 followed. Most countries forbid the import or export of hallucinatory drugs, although many permit the movement of 'soft' drugs.

Different countries have different internal legislation on pornography. Material which can be imported into the Netherlands, for instance, could not legally be imported into the UK.

Internationally there are attempts to prevent the pirating of goods, eg counterfeit Chanel T-shirts made in Hong Kong, or the great number of compact discs and video tapes produced in various locations. Goods which are counterfeited are not only often substandard, they can be positively dangerous as has been tragically demonstrated with vehicle spares.

Protecting selected industries

Trying to prevent counterfeiting obviously protects both the buying public and the general manufacturer. Protection can be more specific eg by insisting that goods must be carried by a nominated carrier which is state owned, or by stipulating subcontractors. An airline might, for example, place an order for aircraft but specify the particular engines to be used.

Protecting currencies

Governments can insist that all contracts are made in a particular currency (normally a 'hard' currency) or by use of Exchange Control Acts restrict the amount which is available or can be brought in or out of the country.

Implementing controls

These controls may be implemented in many ways but the most common are:

- licensing;
- quotas;
- embargoes;
- bureaucracy;

Licensing

In theory all movements of goods are subject to a licence. In the UK this can be either an *open general licence (OGL)* or a *specific licence.*

An OGL permits anyone to export, or import, any of the goods covered by it. In the UK is implemented by Export of Goods (Control) Orders issued from time to time by the Department of Trade and Industry (DTI). Copies of the Order and current amendments can be obtained from Her Majesty's Stationery Office (HMSO). Most other countries have similar procedures.

Specific licences can be issued to an individual company or 'the trade' in general. They are normally valid for either a specific quantity or a period of time. These licences cover a wide range of items from arms, nuclear materials and machine tools to works of art. (UK readers may remember the occasion when a licence was refused to permit the export of a particular painting.)

Fines, delays, seizure of goods, even a gaol sentence could follow the attempt to ship without a licence – so always check!

Quotas

The GATT definition of a quota is 'an agreement between governments which stipulates the amount of a commodity which can be imported into one country from another country'. The exporting country normally controls the system by issuing export licences. Again these can relate to a period of time as well, eg 5000 printed T-shirts, to be shipped between 1 March and 30 May 1996. Under a *dual licensing system* the importing country will require the importer to obtain a specific import licence as well.

Embargoes

The classic definition of an embargo is an order forbidding ships of a foreign power to enter, or any ships to leave, the country's ports – in other words a complete suspension of commercial traffic.

Bureaucracy

In many ways this is the most frustrating restraint: using official processes to slow down trade, or even make it impossible. Classic examples include:

- deciding that all imports of video recorders had to come into France through one specific customs post;
- deciding that European skis were not safe, because Japanese snow had a different flake pattern. The skis could therefore not be used as skis;
- deciding that a liquor did not meet the minimum alcohol content required by German law (the Casis De Dijon case);
- requiring every piece of literature or documentation to be in French.

(In case any UK reader is feeling superior do not forget British rain and its effect on leaves on railway tracks in the South East.)

COLLECTING PAYMENT OF DUTY ON ALL GOODS

In the same way that all goods are theoretically liable to control by Customs and Excise unless exempted by an OGL, all goods are subject to duty unless either:

- the tariff rate is nil; or
- some exemption or suspension has been given.

Duties fall into two categories: *customs duty* which is levied on imports, and *excise duty* which can be levied on both imports and home-produced items. As an *aide-mémoire* it has been said that excise duties are taxes raised by government on the simple pleasures of life, like alcohol, perfume and petrol.

Many countries in the world now use the *harmonised commercial description* and *coding system* (H/S) to describe and classify goods. Against each heading is the appropriate customs tariff. In the UK, for example, there is one tariff for goods from the EU (nil), and others for the rest of the world. It is very important that goods are described in accordance with the tariff. Incorrect descriptions not only cause delay but can cost money. If the customs officer cannot trace the description you have given 'in the book', he or she is quite entitled to enter it as 'others', which needless to say will carry a high rate of duty.

The basic premiss is that any product being imported is potentially subject to duty (which, as mentioned, could be nil) but suspensions can be obtained. To get such an exemption it has to be shown (before the importation) that either there are specific reasons as to why duty should not be charged, even though the goods are going to be used in the importing country, or that the goods are to be re-exported, possibly after some work has taken place on them.

Temporary suspension from duty

Temporary suspension will normally be granted if:

- the goods are not produced in the EU (this only applies to EU member states);
- they are of a specialised nature not obtainable elsewhere.

If the goods or materials will not be sold in the importing country but merely held for re-shipment or processing before re-shipment, duty can be suspended in one of the following ways:

- *Inward processing relief.* Goods imported for processing and subsequent export outside the EU can be relieved of customs and other import duties, but not VAT. Any applicable duty is payable if the goods are re-exported within the EU.
- *End use relief.* Goods are allowed free entry if they are to be used for a specified purpose acceptable under EU regulations.

- *Free ports/free trade zones (FTZ).* There are enclosed areas into which goods may be moved without payment of customs duty or VAT. Duty is only payable if the goods are either consumed within the zone or are taken out into the local market.
- *Approved warehousing.* This is a secure place (eg a bonded warehouse) approved by Customs and Excise for the storage of goods. Duty is not paid until goods leave the warehouse.

With all of these methods of deferring or suspending duty, meticulous records have to be kept and goods are liable to inspection by Customs and Excise at any time.

FURTHER DOCUMENTATION

There are two other major activities which impact on distribution: the movement of goods or vehicles through a country, and the temporary export of items which will not be sold and will eventually return to the exporter.

The first situation, in which goods may cross several national frontiers to reach their ultimate destination, is covered by the *Transport International Routier (TIR)* convention. This is now observed by more than 90 countries. Within the EU *Community Transit* fulfils the same objectives, while samples, exhibition materials, etc, are covered by an *ATA carnet* (normally issued by the appropriate chamber of commerce).

These variations from the straightforward import or export of goods require specific documentation in addition to the normal commercial documentation already mentioned. Apart from carnets and licences the following can typically be required:

- certificate of origin;
- health/phytosanitary/veterinary certificates;
- consular invoice.

Customs duties are levied on the cost of the goods (purchase price, insurance, carriage) at the point at which it enters the country unless provision has been made for clearance at an inland depot. In making a customs entry, the authorities will require at least:

- commercial invoice;
- single administrative document (SAD);
- evidence of freight and insurance charges.

Other documents may be required as indicated earlier to prove that all information given is correct.

The normal procedure is as follows:

- An entry is made on the SAD. This details the description, value, quantity, rate of duty, and various other relevant details about the goods.
- When presented to customs it is accompanied by all relevant support documentation described earlier in this chapter. Customs, at their discretion, will examine the goods. It should be noted that any opening, unpacking and repacking of the goods must be carried out by the importer or agent (who may in some cases be a member of the port authorities staff).
- Assuming that the customs officer is satisfied that the goods are in order he or she certifies the entry form and stamps the *Out of Charge Note (C130)*. The out of charge note authorises the removal of the goods once any duties have been paid.
- It should, of course, be noted that dock dues will have to be paid.

*NB: The procedures described are those followed by HM Customs and Excise. Most countries have similar procedures but **do check first**.*

INTERNATIONAL ORGANISATIONS PROMOTING OR REGULATING TRADE

Most countries have their own organisations to promote trade, after all this is one of the main responsibilities of an embassy, and trade organisations (eg the Society of British Aircraft Constructors) and regional or local authorities (eg the Welsh Development Authority) play their specialised part.

There are, however, three major organisations (or types of organisation) which must be considered. These are:

- trading blocs;
- GATT/WTO;
- the International Chamber of Commerce.

Trading blocs

For many centuries groups of countries have joined together in formal trade agreements. These can range from a simple bilateral agreement to give preference to each other's goods (often by lower tariffs), to a customs union where members charge a common tariff to non-members and the resulting income is spread between them, to the full common market with effectively a common tariff ring fence against non-members, free circulation of goods and services within the market, and an increasing number of common policies. The classic example of this in our lifetime, of course, is the European Union (EU), which is looked at in closer detail in the next chapter.

There are an increasing number of trading blocs in the world, limited either by geography (North American Free Trade Area – NAFTA) or by a common interest (Organisation of Petroleum Exporting Countries – OPEC). Reference to history will demonstrate how powerful – even if only for a relatively short time – some of these bodies can be.

Self-Examination Question

How many trading blocs does your company get involved with? How do they impact on the way you do business?

If the answer is 'not at all' consider the influence of OPEC, particularly in the 1970s.

GATT/WTO

The General Agreement on Tariffs and Trade (GATT) was formed by the United Nations in 1948 with 23 members. By the time it was succeeded by the World Trade Organisation (WTO) at the beginning of 1995 it had grown into an organisation of 124 members with another 20 or more in the pipeline.

The overall aim of GATT was that there should be common free trade between members. This would be achieved by:

- eliminating quota restrictions;
- reducing tariffs progressively by reciprocal negotiation;

- removing restrictive non-tariff barriers to trade;
- ensuring that all countries are treated in the same way (most favoured nation);
- transparency of any remaining protection.

Two important principles were:

- *Article IIA: Most favoured nation (MFN)*. Any concession offered by one country to another must be open to all GATT members.
- *Article VI: Anti dumping*. Dumping occurs when the export price is either less than:
    — that charged in the exporting country's domestic market, or
    — the highest price charged when exporting, or
    — the production costs, plus reasonable selling costs or profit margins, in the exporting country.

    If it is agreed dumping has taken place, the importing country can impose levies (to eliminate the difference) before applying the duties it would have charged under the country's tariff. It can, of course, be difficult to prove that dumping has taken place as the importing country has to prove that its internal market has been disrupted. Nevertheless actions have been taken, or threatened, such as the USA's reaction to imports of cheap European steel.

It was recognised that, given the different economic strengths of the various members, immediate free trade could be counter-productive. Countries were classified into four groups (in descending order of economic viability):

- FICS – Fully Industrialised Countries;
- NICS – Newly Industrialised Countries;
- LDC – Lesser Developed Countries;
- LDDC – Lesser Developed Developing Countries.

Both LDCs and LDDCs were permitted 'Special and Differential Treatment'. Under this they were not obliged to adhere to the principles of reciprocity if they could show it would harm their development, particularly of new industries.

There were also a number of derogations from the general principles.

- *Article XII*: Countries may take measures to protect themselves against payment difficulties.

- *Article XVIII*: LDCs and LDDCs can use protective measures to ensure the effectiveness of a development programme.

- *Article XIX*: Unilateral protectionist measures can be taken by any country if a sudden jump in imports threatens serious injury to domestic products.

In addition to these general derogations provision was made for *Voluntary Restraint Agreements (VRA)* and the *Multi-Fibre Arrangement (MFA)*.

A VRA is a bilateral agreement to restrain trade. A classic example of this was the 1985 microchip agreement between Japan and the USA. Japan agreed that in return for charging 'fair wages' prices to the USA (and other countries) it would ensure that 20 per cent of the market was given to American-owned companies.

The MFA has been referred to by Jack Butler in *The Importer's Handbook* (Woodhead Faulkner, 1994) as 'perhaps the most notorious and comprehensive example of a GATT derogation'. The MFA is a complex subject outside the scope of a general textbook but in essence it gives protection (mainly by means of quotas) to established producers against the developing countries.

It would be easy to assume that GATT had really achieved little, but this is not the case. A series of major negotiating rounds starting with the Dillon round in 1950, culminating in the Uruguay round completed in 1994, have considerably reduced tariffs for manufactured goods. Suggested procedures have been established in such areas as government procurement and many of the EU procurement directives have taken much from GATT.

It has been estimated that the average tariff on manufactured goods fell from 40 per cent in 1947 to 4.7 per cent by 1990 (University of the West of England).

GATT is now in the process of being replaced by the WTO which officially came into being on 1 January 1995. As countries ratify the Uruguay round in their own legislation they will become members of the WTO. The new organisation has a broader remit than GATT, and member states must subscribe to all the agreements and procedures. Decisions will, however, have to be taken by consensus. Major issues on the agenda include trade in services and intellectual property rights. In addition, the agreements already reached to reduce or abolish barriers to agriculture and textiles under the Uruguay round will require detailed supervision.

The WTO also differs from GATT in that there is an appeals tribunal to handle complaints. Failure to comply with tribunal judgements will make a country liable to WTO authorised trade sanctions. The first major complaint, by Venezuela and Brazil against the USA claiming discrimination against imported fuel on environmental grounds, was due a decision by the end of 1995.

Eventually GATT will be wound up as the WTO takes over all its activities.

International Chamber of Commerce (ICC)

The ICC was founded in 1919 and is based in Paris. It represents companies and associations in 139 countries.

The role of the ICC is to promote the growth of international trade and industry by integrating the business community's approach to progress and problems.

The ICC provides many services to the trading community. Reference has already been made to INCOTERMS – the standard terms of trade used in import/export control. In addition the ICC is the author of the standard reference on the use of LOCs (ICC Booklet number 500 *Uniform Customs and Practice for Documentary Credits*). ATA carnets which allow goods to be temporarily imported duty free were originated by the ICC, and it was also instrumental in drafting model regulations to harmonise guarantees on major construction projects.

The ICC is also responsible for coordinating the activities of the International Court of Arbitration. A recent example of their involvement was in the dispute between Eurotunnel and the British and French rail authorities.

Finally the ICC is involved in setting guidelines for an international ethical code for business.

SUMMARY

This chapter has looked at the major requirements for documentation and control that lie behind every transaction.

It has considered the role of Customs and Excise and the work being done by the international bodies active in this area.

This is, by its nature, a constantly changing scene as far as detail is concerned and readers are advised to contact either their local chamber of commerce, the DTI or a freight forwarder (see Appendix 7) for the up-to-date situation on any product or country.

Suggested specialist reading

Butler, J B (1994) *The Importer's Handbook*, Woodhead Faulkner.

Downs, D E (1992) *Understanding the Freight Business,* Micor Freight UK.

ICC INCOTERMS 1990, ICC Publishing SA.

SITPRO, 29 Glasshouse Street, London W1R 5RG (various publications on documentation and procedures).

Trade and International Banking Services, Services for Importer and Exporter, Midland Bank plc.

Chapter 8

DISTRIBUTION INSIDE THE EUROPEAN UNION

OUTLINE

This chapter considers the specific problems and the opportunities for rationalising distribution brought about by the development of the European Union. It addresses three main topics:

- VAT and INTRASTAT implications for distribution;
- EU legislation;
- the creation and development of European distribution networks.

INTRODUCTION

In Chapter 7 consideration was given to the major problems of documentation and authorisation facing distribution globally. In this chapter attention is concentrated on some of the specific problems relating to members of the EU, many of which also lie in the area of documentation. As is so often the case in tackling any problem, it helps to mentally stand back and review how the situation developed, and the concepts that lay behind it.

The European Economic Community (EEC) from which the EU has developed, came into being on 1 January 1958 following the signing of the Treaty of Rome in 1957 by France, West Germany, (now Germany), Italy, The Netherlands, Belgium and Luxembourg. The original objectives were:

- to create a customs union with common tariffs against non-members;
- to dismantle tariffs and quotas between member states;

- to identify and remove non-tariff barriers to trade between member states;
- to establish a Common Agricultural Policy (CAP);
- to agree arrangements for dealing with member states' colonial dependencies (and countries with which they had a special relationship, ie former colonies and client states).

Over the years other states have applied for, and obtained, membership: the UK, Denmark and the Republic of Ireland in the 1970s; Greece, Portugal and Spain in the 1980s; and most recently Finland, Sweden and Austria. Many of the former Eastern Bloc countries are in various stages of moving towards possible eventual membership, so that one day there could well be a community stretching, in the celebrated quote, from the Atlantic to the Urals.

As the body has grown in size so have the objectives. The single European Act of 1986 adopted several proposals in preparation for the creation of a European Union far beyond the bounds of a purely customs union. The Act covers areas such as:

- economic and social congruency;
- environmental issues (see Chapter 9);
- political cooperation;
- institutional cooperation.

The concept of the level playing field is often maligned (more for its absence) but at least in theory there should be complete freedom of movement, and equality of opportunity, for any activity involving the nationals of any of the member states. Gradually the barriers to the movement of goods and services, including finance, are disappearing as protectionism is phased out, but many still exist.

VAT AND INTRASTAT

On 1 January 1993 two important changes were made in the EU following the 'completion' of the Single Market. These have a major impact on business and concern:

- the charging and accounting of VAT for goods moving between member states;
- the method of collecting trade statistics for these groups.

The changes have major implications for the trader or for someone act-ing as agent on his or her behalf. Full details can be found in *HM Customs and Excise Notices 60 and 725.*

VAT

One of the effects of the 1 January 1993 changeover was that all internal EU trade is carried out on a *destination system* insofar as VAT is concerned. In HM Customs and Excise Notice 725 it states:

> A transaction involving the movement of goods between EU member states is treated for VAT purposes as a supply of goods in the member state from which the goods are despatched. For most of those supplies between VAT registered traders in different member states, VAT need not be charged on despatch. It is, however, due from the customer on acquisition of the goods concerned in the member state to which they are delivered.
>
> For supplies of goods to customers in other EU states who are not registered for VAT, tax is normally charged and accounted for by the VAT registered supplier in the member state from which the goods are despatched.

As with domestic trade the trader must show on his or her VAT sales invoice the customer VAT registration number.

Self-Examination Question

Do you know the VAT numbers of your customers? Is it shown on their documentation?

At the beginning of 1997 the procedure will change, in theory, to an *origin system.* This, of course, implies that by then there will be a common rate, or rates, for VAT in the EU.

There is one final major factor to be borne in mind, and that is the principle of *triangulation.* HM Customs and Excise define this as:

> a chain of supplies or goods involving three parties when, instead of the goods physically passing from one party to the next, they are delivered directly from the first party to the last in the chain.

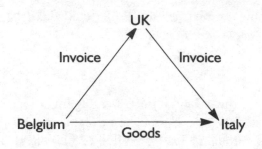

Figure 8.1 *Triangulation*

As an example in Figure 8.1, a UK company receives an order from a company in Italy, which they meet by shipping goods from their own third-party supplier or associate company in Belgium. While there are, in theory, movements between Belgium and the UK, and the UK and Italy, there is only one physical movement of goods – Belgium to Italy.

Not all states handle this movement in the same way for VAT purposes. The Netherlands, for instance, may insist that you have an office in the intervening country. You must check with your local customs, chamber of commerce or freight forwarder.

NB: This is in fact quite a complex subject. Readers who are likely to be practically involved are recommended to obtain copies of Notice 60 and Notice 725 from their local VAT office of HM Customs and Excise.

INTRASTAT (Inter-Community Trade Statistics)

Any country, or, in the case of a common market, group of countries, needs to know what goods are coming into the country or area, and what are going out. Traditionally this collection of information was one of the responsibilities of Customs and Excise, in their role of the goods recording department of the country. You will recall, from the section on Customs and Excise in Chapter 7, that in the process of making a customs entry, the trader had to give a full description of the goods, referenced by the uniform customs tariff.

Since 1 January 1993, all entries in respect of goods are the responsibility of the trader. The document used is the *VAT return*, or if a larger business, by the *supplementary declaration*. Under UK law the trader is guilty of a criminal offence if incorrect or incomplete information is provided. The information can be supplied either manually or by IT (HM Customs and Excise, as in other areas, are encouraging the use of IT).

Thresholds which determine how information is to be provided are normally reviewed at the year end, but it should be noted that some states have thresholds as low as £10,000 (or their domestic currency equivalent).

EU LEGISLATION

The purpose of EU legislation is to facilitate the creation of a truly common market with a completely barrier-free interchange of goods and services within member states. Any national custom or practice which could be considered to raise a barrier to such movement is subject to modification or prohibition, unless a member state specifically opts out. As an illustration; as from 1 October 1995 in the UK it was no longer legally acceptable to sell packaged goods other than by metric weight, and penalties could be exacted for non-compliance.

These rules and regulations affect all aspects of commercial life, and logically stem from the Treaty of Rome 1957 and the Single European Act 1986. These effectively set out the basic requirements of the EU, and are expanded and detailed in various ways. All member states are required to embody the provisions of the Single European Act in their own domestic legislation, so that any infringement is an infringement of their national law, and the responsibility for enforcement lies within the individual member country.

Legislative measures take four forms:

- Regulations;
- Directives;
- Decisions;
- Recommendations.

Regulations are laws binding to all member states. They are the highest category and no national laws are required to enforce them. A good example of this is EC Regulation 3820/85 which covers the number of drivers' hours permissible.

Directives define end objectives, but put the onus on individual member states to implement them. Most of the business community will be aware of the various procurement Directives which specify the procedure to be followed when public money is spent. Examples are the Supplies, the Public Works and the Services and Utilities Directives. (NB: The Utilities Directive also affects the privatised utility companies in the UK.)

Decisions are similar in application to Regulations, but relate to individual countries, as against blanket legislation.

Recommendations are not binding but often give a pointer to future legislation.

Key articles in the Treaty of Rome were:

- *Article 85*: Power to control any agreement between undertakings which may result in the prevention, restriction or distortion of competition.
- *Article 86*: Power to prohibit use of dominant positions.
- *Article 91*: Extends the operation of Articles 85 and 86 to any action by member states whereby either public or private enterprises are given exclusive or special rights.

As has already been stated, the objectives were to create a completely discrimination-free internal market with no barriers to open competition. Some typical differences in the distribution field were:

- permitted drivers' hours;
- speed limits;
- weight, size and capacity restrictions;
- border formalities;
- cabotage.

Cabotage is the process by which (originally) trade in territorial waters was restricted to ships of that nationality thus protecting domestic carriers. It was then extended to cover the movement of any goods within a country so that, for example, a German haulier delivering goods in the UK could not carry a load back to Germany but would have to run empty.

The majority of these problems have now been resolved, but in the UK we still drive on the left-hand side of the road, and have a lower weight limit on the capacity of a vehicle. Some border crossings, eg going into Italy, can still be time consuming.

Once again, do not assume that all countries are identical. *Check first.*

THE CREATION AND DEVELOPMENT OF EUROPEAN DISTRIBUTION NETWORKS

Take 15 countries, most with long-established frontiers and different historical and commercial perspectives, throw them into the melting pot of the EU, and what do you get at the practical level? In so far as distribution is concerned the result is a series of, in many cases, disconnected activities which have somehow to be brought together in a homogenous whole. There is an apocryphal saying to describe the situation: 'You wouldn't start from here in the first place.'

To be brought together are the airlines, some of which are private companies but many are state owned or were formerly state controlled; the railways, which in mainland Europe are mainly state owned (NB Directive 91/440 requires the management of national railways to be separated from the management of train operations); the shipping companies, most of which are private although some receive subsidies; and road transport, which is primarily in the hands of private operators. Considering the infrastructure there is again a mixed picture. The road and rail networks are generally in the public sector (although charging mechanisms can differ). Airports and seaports can be both private and public (local authority or national government). Communication systems are often at least state influenced. To underscore the whole setup the legal and financial institutions still reflect the historical culture and customs of the individual countries and can be quite different.

Distribution companies have grown mainly by taking over other companies which had to operate within these complexities, and overall strategies and systems are only gradually being introduced. Attempts to speed up the development of genuine integrated networks are being driven by two main sources:

- the commercial impact of the major suppliers and customers of distribution services;

- the rationalisation of the major state or semi-state owned providers, particularly of infrastructure.

Although a relatively small land mass, Europe is 'home' to some of the biggest multinationals in the world eg, Shell, Unilever, Siemens, Philips, Nestlé, ABB, etc. These companies think globally, move goods globally and increasingly look for one company to provide the distribution service. In June 1995 the Compaq Computer Corporation announced plans to disband its previous network of warehouses located in individual countries and concentrate on three centres in the UK, France and the Netherlands. Operating responsibility for all three countries was to be given to one service provider, with the delivery of goods to another. Texas Instruments have gone even further, and handle 90 per cent of the distribution of their European sales from one centre in Utrecht (Netherlands), using one company to manage the operation on its behalf.

The other motivation is being generated by the providers themselves, with considerable support in some instances from the EU. This is probably best illustrated by the so-called Trans-European Network (TEN). Under this a considerable amount of work is taking place which, among other activities, will:

- develop high speed combined road/rail links between:
  — Rotterdam and the Ruhr;
  — Lyons and Turin;
  — the Brenner Tunnel (Austria/Italy);

- develop high speed rail links between:

  — Paris–Brussels–Cologne–Amsterdam–London (using the Channel tunnel);
  — Madrid–Barcelona–Perpignan;
  — Paris–Metz–Strasbourg–Mannheim;
  — Munich–Nuremburg–Leipzig–Berlin.

The EU itself does not get involved in these projects but via *PACT (Programme of Assistance for Combined Transport)* it funds studies, market research and trials. Most readers will be aware of work that has been done on trunk roads with the assistance of the EU, particularly when this is helping to open up outlying areas.

This leads into another problem facing distribution. Population and industry are not uniformly spread. It has been estimated that over three-fifths of the population lives, and three-fifths of the combined Gross National Product is produced, in the so-called *golden triangle*. A triangle with its base on the line Paris–Cologne, with its apex in Glasgow, accounts for more than 25 per cent of the EU's total sales. Within this triangle 'nothing is more than a day away', outside it can be at least two/three days and probably more–depending on the number of transshipments. An overlay of the existing road, rail and air routes would show the same basic concentration in the golden triangle with relatively isolated pockets of activity away from this core.

One of the objectives of the Trans-European Network is to link peripheral countries like Portugal and Greece, and the South of Italy, with the centre. Another objective is to reduce the congestion within the triangle. It has been estimated by the OECD that this costs 2 per cent of gross national product.

SUMMARY

This chapter has concentrated on some of the problems and possibilities stemming from the creation of the European Union.

It started with the historical background and then looked at the unique problem of administering VAT across national frontiers and the allied problem of INTRASTAT.

Consideration was then given to some of the legislation enacted by the EU to achieve a level playing field for all members.

Finally it looked at the pressures leading to the formation of European distribution networks.

Suggested specialist reading

Dudley, J W (1993) *1993 and Beyond: New Strategies for the Emerging Single Market*, Kogan Page.

Chapter 9

ENVIRONMENTAL CONSIDERATIONS

OUTLINE

This chapter looks at the growth in EU and UK environmental legislation and the reasons for this.

It then considers the problems of collection, recycling and disposal of goods and packaging.

Finally it examines controls and costs, and the impact these have on distribution routes and times.

THE GROWTH IN EU AND UK LEGISLATION

'Concern for the environment is the growth industry of the 1990s.' This, possibly cynical, statement reflects the change in acceptable practice and social and political expectation, that has taken place, with gathering momentum, towards the end of the twentieth century. Practices which were perfectly normal in the 1960s and 1970s would now risk at the very least a fine under civil law, and possibly a custodial sentence under criminal law.

Environmental problems interact whether we are at work, rest or play, and include concepts such as:

- pollution;
- health and safety;
- public interest;
- conservation;
- protection.

Nearly all are questions of degree, and tend to become politicised. Somebody who has been out of work for a year might not object to working in a glue factory, but the person who lives next door to the factory probably would not like the smell and might well complain to the Environmental Health Officer! Undoubtedly your view of Heathrow, or any other large airport, is influenced by whether you happen to live under the main flight path.

There is now an increasing body of legislation, provision for public inquiry and role for the local Environmental Health Officer impacting on the operation of a distribution business, starting with thinking about building a warehouse and ending with the customer using the final product. A book could probably be written on this subject alone but some of the main issues are briefly considered below.

The warehouse

Relevant issues to consider here include:

- planning permission;
- operator licensing system;
- conditions of work;
- hazardous goods regulations;
- pollution.

Under the 1968 Transport Act as amended by the 1982 Transport Act: 'Owners and occupiers of land in the vicinity of the (operating) centre may object if the use of the centre would prejudicially affect their use of, or enjoyment of, their land.'

When the buildings are ready for occupation do they provide an appropriate working environment for all who come onto the premises? Legislation to be considered includes:

- The Health and Safety at Work Act 1979;
- The Offices, Shops and Railway Premises Act 1963;
- The Electricity at Work Regulations 1989;
- The Occupier's Liability Act 1957.

Running through all of these is the concept of *duty of care* which requires the occupier/employer (or his or her employees) to take all reasonable precautions to ensure the safety of anybody, employee or member of the public, who comes onto the premises or mode of transport, be it legally or, in the case of trespass, illegally.

The actual operating hours of the building could well be affected by local environmental by-laws, ranging from the noise arising from the use of machinery to the congestion caused by vehicles entering or leaving the premises. Two important laws in this connection are the Environmental Noise and Statutory Nuisance Acts 1990 and 1994.

Most of the UK Acts have their counterparts in other EU countries. Once again, however, the only sensible course to follow is to check the prevailing circumstances in the specific country.

Transit

Relevant issues to consider here include:

- working hours;
- licensing;
- emission;
- routeings.

When goods are actually placed in transit legislation covers both the 'crew' of the transit medium and the general public in the areas through which the aircraft, ship, train or vehicle passes.

Legislation covering the 'crew' details such items as permitted hours of work, rest periods, intervals between blocks of work, etc. An increasing amount of legislation covers the fitness of the individual to carry out the work, ranging from medical tests to examinations of competence. Airline pilots, ships' masters and lorry drivers all need to be 'licensed' to operate their particular craft or vehicle, and a significant percentage of the work of any police force is concerned with the roadworthiness of vehicles and drivers.

An increasing area of environmental concern is the discharge, accidental or otherwise, of unacceptable materials from transport. This can range from a major oil spillage from a supertanker to rubbish falling off a lorry. By far the most significant, as far as the public is concerned, is the emission of vehicle exhausts.

The Royal Commission on Environmental Pollution (*Transport and the Environment,* Com 2674, HMSO) reported in 1994 that 'If current trends were to be maintained the levels of pollution and congestion would become unacceptable.' They agreed that if emissions were to be reduced to 1990 levels by 2000:

- fuel efficiency would have to be significantly increased;
- speed limits would have to be more rigorously enforced;
- car use in urban areas would have to be halved;
- fuel prices would have to be doubled in real terms.

Self-Examination Question

If the Royal Commission's Report were to be fully implemented, how would this affect your distribution strategy?

Transport is also regulated to reduce its impact on the environment in other ways. Initially these restrictions were purely related to safety, examples being weight restrictions on bridges or minor roads and width or height restrictions on roads or under bridges. Increasingly there is now legislation to specify routes which must be followed, as instanced by the procedures covering the movement of nuclear waste, and the times when routes can be used. In Germany there is now a campaign to restrict goods movements to the hours of darkness only, while in many UK towns heavy goods vehicles can only load/unload between midnight and 06.00.

These regulations again can significantly affect the way distribution can be carried out. From the purely business point of view the matters discussed in this chapter could well result in longer journey times, less frequent deliveries and the possible resiting of facilities, culminating in higher transport costs.

Any alteration to any part of the distribution chain, be it of goods or people, can have far-reaching effects. How will the tunnel under the English Channel affect air flights and ferry traffic? At the time of writing it is too early to say, but fears have already been expressed that any real improvement in rail/road transport times will impact on the profitable short-haul air transport business (which some people claim to be the worst offender in terms of energy usage).

Delivery

Relevant issues to consider here include:

- customer requirements;
- returns;
- recycling.

Your customers want reliable deliveries and less stocks; they do not want their employees or their customers to be put at risk; they do not want the problems of getting rid of packaging. All customers, quite reasonably, want to avoid trouble with their Environmental Health Officer.

In addition to the problems and legislation already mentioned there are two other major controls in the UK:

- the Control of Substances Hazardous to Health (COSHH) Regulations 1988;
- the HAZCHEM system.

Local authorities also have it within their remit to influence the sale and home distribution of certain products in their area of jurisdiction. This can lead to the apparent anomaly of a county supplies organisation being permitted to sell a product outside its own area, but not within it!

Once again, the manager has to check that what is being planned, or currently taking place, is still legal. Because a practice is acceptable at the point of loading does not mean it is acceptable at the point of distribution, particularly if this is in another country (see also Appendix 8: procedure for transporting dangerous goods).

THE PROBLEMS OF COLLECTION, RECYCLING AND DISPOSAL

Waste, and the management of waste disposal, is another issue which now materially affects distribution but which would hardly have been considered 20 years ago.

Until comparatively recently the job of distribution was just to get goods to the customer. Unless the products were on, or in, something which was considered to have a reuse value, that was that. The customer took responsibility for the disposal of waste packaging (cardboard, bottles, shrink wrap, film, drums, packing cases, etc). Legislation, such as the UK

Environmental Protection Act 1990, The Duty of Care Regulations 1992 and the EU Packaging Waste Directives, have accelerated the change which has gained momentum since the 1970s.

The Duty of Care Regulations 1992 require all producers, keepers, carriers and disposers of waste to take sufficient steps to ensure the proper disposal of waste. Such care includes proper containment, labelling and description of wastes and detailed documentation and transfer to appropriately qualified companies.

The EU Packaging Waste Directives, in their present format, will require that by 2001:

- between 50 and 65 per cent of packaging must be recovered annually rather than be sent for use as landfill;
- between 25 and 45 per cent of packaging must be recycled.

In this context it is worth noting the increased fears now being expressed at the capacity of landfill sites to generate explosive and or toxic gases.

Reduce, recycle and reuse are now the guidelines for packaging designers. It is interesting to note, for instance, the increasing share of the household washing and cleaning products market which is now being taken by smaller packs of concentrated materials.

This is all still an emerging area and the reader is advised to keep informed by means of the regular updates on this subject which appear in the trade and business press. If a distribution activity wishes to remain competitive then it will have to adapt to changing circumstances which may well cause a complete reversal of previous policies.

The Chicago Exchange, it is reported, is now beginning to deal even in contracts for 'waste' materials!

THE FUTURE

Crystal ball gazing can well be an exercise in today's headlines and tomorrow's oblivion, but unless there is a complete change in the public attitude to the environment it is not beyond the realms of possibility that in the future environmental considerations will have an even greater impact on business in general and distribution in particular. These influences will possibly be greatest in the fields of:

- energy saving and control;
- environmental protection;
- traffic congestion.

Energy saving and control

In the period 1969–88 world consumption of primary energy increased by 64 per cent. Hidden within this figure is the fact that consumption in South East Asia rose by 396 per cent. Population growth and the pressure for higher living standards in the developing world, and the tendency to more and smaller households in the developed world, will cause this growth to continue.

The first law of thermodynamics states that energy can neither be created nor destroyed, although its distribution can change. Energy is a finite resource and it is therefore predictable that increasing attempts will be made, both nationally and internationally, to control its use and make its consumption more efficient. This is emphasised by the work which is being done to make internal combustion engines more efficient. The 'gas guzzler' is now considered antisocial and much legislation favours the vehicle with the smaller engine. In the USA the state of California has tabled a requirement that 2 per cent of 1998-model sales must be zero-emission vehicles and by 2003 this must have risen to 10 per cent.

Is it too far-fetched to consider that the trend towards 'park and ride' in private travel will extend commercially, that there will be collecting points serving each conurbation and deliveries/collections within the conurbation boundary will be carried out by energy efficient light transport?

In the 1970s the western world gave a knee-jerk reaction to the OPEC oil embargo, rationing petroleum-based fuels; energy crises arising from shortages of electricity in the UK were effectively dealt with again by rationing and allocation to priority users. Could not similar measures take place once more but on a permanent basis? In the UK there has been a significant change to the use of unleaded petrol, helped by differential pricing and excise duty. Worldwide there is a noticeable lobby in favour of road pricing regulating the usage and size of vehicles.

Environmental protection

There are already more than 100 EU Directives concerned with controlling and monitoring the implementation of environmental policy and legislation in member states. They cover such varied topics as air pollution, chemical controls, conservation and special protection areas, energy, fuels and transport, industrial plants, waste and water quality. The list is constantly being added to.

NIMBY – 'Not in My Back Yard' – has gone into the index of standard British mnemonics. Similar attitudes exist in other countries, some of whom might feel they have been exploited in the past by, among others, multinational companies.

All of these, and the other factors discussed above will tend to increase costs and may well be used to create a barrier against outside competition.

Traffic congestion

The Straits of Dover, air traffic corridors and major orbital motorways all have one thing in common. At certain times they jam up solid. In any large city the ripple effect of congestion is immediate and far reaching. How much do we want to allocate to new runways, 8/10 lane motorways, new rail links, etc? And will it really make any difference? On many flights the waiting time at either end, and the transit time in getting to and from the airport, is greater than the journey time.

The Freight Transport Association calculated that congestion cost the UK £25 million in 1994. How will all this modify the greater use of 'just in time' techniques? The debate continues; watch this space.

SUMMARY

This chapter brings the reader up to date in considering the result of environmental pressures on all that has been achieved so far in distribution.

It has looked at the type of legislation that is increasingly being tabled and the reasons for it. Next the problem of recycling and waste disposal was examined.

Finally an attempt was made to explore some of the ways in which the future could require change, and the challenge this presents.

Suggested specialist reading

Consult current surveys in *The Financial Times* and the fortnightly publication of the Chartered Institute of Purchasing and Supply. See also: Simpson, S (1990) *The Times Guide to the Environment,* Times Books.

Chapter 10

MEASURING AND CONTROLLING PERFORMANCE

OUTLINE

In this chapter reference is made to some of the commonly used techniques of performance evaluation:

- predetermined standards;
- interfirm comparison;
- benchmarking;
- direct product profitability (DPP).

WHY MEASURE?

'Beauty', it is said, 'lies in the eye of the beholder.' Performance, by the same token, must be the perception of the third-party customers and not just the company management. In running a business there are several customers to consider. There are the customers, in the orthodox sense, who buy the product or service. There are also the customers, in the broadest sense of the link in the chain, who provide – or withdraw – the resources which keep the company in existence as a viable entity: the financial community (both institutions and individual shareholders), the staff who man the business, the suppliers of goods and services, and the local and national authorities who regulate the business. As has been discussed in the preceding chapter this last group have an increasingly marked impact on what an organisation does and the way in which it does it.

Before considering any of the evaluation techniques it is first necessary to determine what activities should be measured, why they are
being measured, and what the attributes are by which these different
groups of customers will judge performance.

In a short article published in *Purchasing and Supply Management* in
February 1990 the author described a rough-cut profiling method,
devised by him and one of his then colleagues, David Coppock, which in
a convenient and readily understood manner gave snapshots both of
existing relationships and the way in which they could be improved.
Customers were asked to respond, on a 0–10 scale, on how important a
particular range of activities was to them, and how well these activities
were performed. As a check the 'provider' was asked to complete a similar questionnaire. When the questionnaires were tabulated and the resulting grids (customers and providers) superimposed, the matches and
mismatches were clearly highlighted.

It is surprising how many times the result of such a study is the discovery that the provider is putting a lot of effort into an activity which
the customer is not particularly troubled by, and little into an area which
the customer considers vitally important.

In the UK the privatised utilities have found that performance criteria
took on a completely new meaning. The financial community, as an
example, were very interested in measures like sales per employee.

Any measure must be relevant, timely and not capable of misinterpre-
tation. One measure, on its own, tells very little, and any monitoring
process depends on a correctly targeted battery of measures. To illustrate
the point, stock turnround means little unless linked to levels of service.
In the same way an increase in picks per employee means little if this is
only achieved by doubling the individual's working hours.

Measuring can basically be done in two ways: against predetermined
standards, or against the performance of other organisations.

PREDETERMINED STANDARDS

Standards have been concisely defined as 'any specification intended for
repeated use'. They may be developed externally, by the relevant trade,
national or international bodies, or they may be unique to the specific
organisation, for example a standard price. Depending on the originator

they may have the power of legislation behind them, or they may be entirely voluntary. Or they could have the power of custom and practice behind them. A company does not have to have European Standard EN ISO 9000 to compete on an international basis. On the other hand, many companies will make this a prerequisite to putting a potential supplier onto a tender list. Every company then seeking quality accreditation must have a purchasing procedure which examines the quality policies of its suppliers.

Once standards have been set, monitoring can take place. This can be by an outside body or by members of the company. Again, taking EN ISO 9000, a company will be assessed by an outside body to determine whether or not it meets awarding criteria. On the other hand, if the standard is an internal one, for example the time taken to load a 20 ft container, the measurement will probably be taken by internal staff. In either case the manager will know whether or not a preset standard is being achieved and if there are any variances.

The monthly operating budget statement is a good example of the use of internal standards to monitor and control performance. If there is a variance an investigation will be carried out to determine why and what action should be taken to correct it. Standards give a level, but it can be argued that they give a minimum level of what has to be achieved to comply with preset rules.

They do not, therefore, in themselves, lead to any improvement once the base level has been reached, unless there is a continuous process of review. Equally they give no ready comparison with best practice. Taking an analogy from sport, if a runner reduces his or her time for the 100 metres from 20 seconds to 15 seconds that may be a reduction of 25 per cent, but the athlete is still not world class.

INTER-FIRM COMPARISON

Competition is all about improving standards and hopefully doing better than other organisations. Standards can be improved by the edict of 'every year we will reduce stock by 5 per cent' (or something similar). Which is fine (maybe) until the discovery is made that competitors have reduced theirs by 10 per cent.

The trade magazine *The Grocer* from time to time publishes league tables comparing the stock turnround of various companies operating in the UK food retailing sector. In January they published an analysis by stockturn and days of stock of the 11 major supermarket chains. This indicated that some companies were effectively working on half the stock carried by their competitors.

Many years ago the concept of *interfirm comparison* was developed. Organisations, either working in the same type of business or who were faced with similar problems, sent information against selected parameters to a central independent point. This information was then analysed and fed back in an anonymous form to subscribing members. One classic example of this was in the area of salaries. Companies fed in information of the job levels, salary scales and locations to, in this case, a consultancy which processed the information and published salary scales indexed by job level and location. If I was running a medium-sized transport company in North Wales and wanted to recruit a warehouse manager I could find out the average, upper quartile and lower quartile salary that I would probably have to pay.

Another example is (or was) the electricity supply industry. The logistics director in regional electricity company A could find out the average stock turnround by product group for the rest of the RECs.

Much of the statistical information produced by the DTI is of this nature, giving the manager an overall average target. This is obviously helpful but the relatively recent development of the concept of benchmarking takes the process further.

BENCHMARKING

Benchmarking has been defined as 'an approach to continual improvement, by comparing the company's performance with the very best in any industry, and then adopting better business processes wherever this would benefit the company'. As Alan Rushton says in *Logistics and Distribution Planning*, (Kogan Page, 1994): 'The intention [is] to identify the reasons why a certain operation is the best and to establish ways and means of emulating the operation.'

The significant change in this approach is that benchmarking is basically looking not so much at the result, but at the way the result was achieved. What is the process? Is it transferable? Manufacturing and retailing are different, but each can learn from the other. Running an examination syllabus programme has quite a few aspects in common with using MRP1 to solve production control problems. Both involve customers and components on a time-phased basis.

Self-Examination Question

How would you set up a benchmarking project?

The accepted methodology for doing this is as follows:

1. Select a process you want to improve, eg order processing, order picking, vehicle scheduling.
2. Select a project team. Ideally the project leader should be the owner of the process. The team should be cross-functional. (Some of the biggest breakthroughs come from people who do not know you can't do it that way!)
3. Study the process.
4. Develop a set of measures to enable comparisons to be made. (In the example given under point 1 a measure could be elapsed time from receiving an order to raising internal documentation.)
5. Look for companies to benchmark with.
6. Visit and investigate, and communicate result.
7. Produce action plan.
8. Communicate and implement.

In the UK the Department of Trade and Industry has sponsored the development of network groups which operate as best practice clubs in the areas of distribution, purchasing and production. Members come from various sectors of industry and commerce and share experiences and solutions. Member companies have made quite significant break-throughs in improving their management and operations processes and hence reducing time and costs.

DIRECT PRODUCT PROFITABILITY

Writing in the American publication *Distribution* in 1985, Denis Davis made the following comment:

DPP takes the gross margin and refines it into a net contribution for a particular product. It starts by assigning backhaul allowances, promotional allowances, or display allowances then it subtracts the costs attributable to the product, including space, handling costs and refrigeration.

More recently Rushton and Oxley, in *Handbook of Logistics and Distribution Management* (Kogan Page, 1991), defined DPP as a technique of allocating all the appropriate costs and allowances to a given product.

As in any area of accounting the allocation of indirect costs can be very much a matter of opinion. Nonetheless many managers feel that used intelligently DPP can be a very useful tool in deciding:

● What is the best way to move products?
● Are distribution channels appropriate?
● Is there a point beyond which delivery becomes uneconomical?

INFORMATION TECHNOLOGY

This chapter has concentrated on methods of measuring and controlling performance; and it is as well to reinforce the statements made in Chapter 4 that measures must be accurate, timely and constant.

The information that at any one time would have been gathered and processed by an army of clerks can now be collected speedily and accurately (providing data capture is correct) by IT. In many areas of this book the use of IT has been mentioned, and it is fitting to end this chapter with a further comment.

An article in *The Financial Times* by Claire Gooding published on 4 October 1995 was headed 'IT helps deliver goods'. IT, sensibly applied, has made it possible to speed up process times, improve the accuracy of information and reduce stocks. It has also probably aided the development of the concept of an integrated function which, by abolishing former boundaries and the resulting internal delays, can bring additional profit to the business.

SUMMARY

At the start of this chapter the need for accurate and timely information was underlined.

The use of information in measuring and controlling performance, both from internal and external sources, was then described.

The chapter ends by again stressing the need for good IT backup.

Suggested specialist reading

Consult current surveys in *The Financial Times* and the fortnightly publication of the Chartered Institute of Purchasing and Supply.

GLOSSARY

ABC analysis See *Pareto analysis.*

Added value Adding to the product one or more key characteristics which give increased value to the buyer. This value may be real, or merely perceived, but either way it makes the potential customer want to buy a specific product, to the exclusion of other brands or models.

ADR Accord Dangeroux Routier – see Chapter 2.

ATA Carnet Internationally accepted document which covers the temporary import, without duty being paid, of commercial samples, exhibits for international trade fairs and professional equipment.

Backload Term normally used in road transport, although it can be used for any other method of shipment.

Backloading is the principle of making sure that, as far as possible, the carrier never runs empty, and that every journey is at least producing some income.

A classic example was the so-called 'triangle of trade'. UK-based ships took trade goods to West Africa, then transported slaves from West Africa to the West Indies. They then brought back sugar to the UK. On no leg of the journey was the ship empty of cargo.

Back order The situation which occurs when a customer orders an item that is not in stock; the order is filled when this item becomes available. Almost certainly this will incur additional costs – packing, transport, invoicing – none of which can be passed on to the customer.

Channel (as in distribution channel) Method by which a product and/or its legal ownership is transferred from one party to another.

Closed loop A continuous cycle of activities, in which every action/transaction leads into another. There are, therefore, no loose ends.

Co-maker See *partnership (sourcing)*.

Competitive advantage A competitive situation in which a company can (a) gain a relative advantage through measures its competitors will find hard to follow, and (b) extend that advantage further.

Consignment stock Stock dedicated to a specific customer, and quite often stored on the customer's premises. It remains the property of the supplier until drawn off by the customer. At that point the customer will be invoiced for the quantity taken.

It differs from *imprest stock* in that, as drawings are made, the stock is not replenished.

Consolidation Collecting together smaller consignments to form a larger quantity in order to obtain lower freight rates, by dispatching as one shipment. See also *groupage*.

Containerisation Packing goods in box units, normally manufactured to dimensions specified by the International Standards Organisation (ISO). The items contained can then be moved as one unit.

Corporate strategy The overall business strategy detailing the definition of the business, the corporate mission, the direction for development and resource allocation, and the specification of financial objectives.

Cross docking Supplying products from various sources to the distribution warehouse just in time for them to be consolidated, with other products destined for the same customer and shipped out immediately.

Customer service Timeliness and reliability in getting goods and services to the customer in accordance with the customer's expectations.

DGN (Dangerous Goods Note) A clearly distinguishable document printed in red on a white background with a hatched edge. This document, which should accompany all shipments of dangerous goods, gives all relevant details, including the UN identifying number, for the product.

Double handling A process to be avoided! It is a situation where goods have to be handled more than once, without adding value. An example would be taking goods off one lorry, putting them into store for a temporary period, and then putting them onto another lorry for delivery.

DRP1 (Distribution Requirements Planning) A system which takes the forecast demand for finished products at the point of demand, and from this derives time-phased requirements for each level in the system.

DRP2 (Distribution Resource Planning) A system which creates a model of the distribution process in planning the key resources, as they may be affected by different inputs. It is normally considered to encompass:

- sales planning;
- distribution requirements planning (DRP1);
- shipping planning;
- distribution capacity planning and control;
- shipping arrangements.

DTI Department of Trade and Industry (UK only).

EDI (Electronic Data Interchange) The computer-to-computer transfer of commercial or administrative transactions, using an agreed standard to structure the transaction or message data.

Electronic Mail Using computers to communicate messages saving time and paperwork.

EPOS (Electronic Point of Sale) Use of equipment (normally a laser scanner) to collect and store information relating to sales. The scanner reads off the bar code on the article.

It can also provide printed information for the customer. Used originally in supermarkets some companies are now beginning to use EPOS-type systems to record and document stores issues and line counts.

EU (European Union) 'An area without internal frontiers in which the free movement of goods, persons, services and capital is ensured': Article 13, Single European Act.

Previously known as the European Economic Community (EEC) and the European Community (EC), the EU currently (1995) consists of Austria, Belgium, Denmark, Finland, France, Germany, Greece, Ireland, Italy, Luxembourg, the Netherlands, Portugal, Spain, Sweden and the UK.

Exception reports Reports, nowadays normally generated by a computer, listing variances from a pre-set standard or cut-off. An example would be a listing of all journey times taking 10 per cent more or less from a pre-calculated figure.

FTZ (Free Trade Zone) A designated enclosed area where goods and materials may be stored, processed or repacked without payment of duty. Duties only become payable when goods move into the hinterland surrounding the zone.

GATT (General Agreement on Tariffs and Trade) Forum, established in 1948, for the liberalisation of world trade.

Goods flow The movement of goods and materials (and the accompanying documentation) through the organisation, from the moment the customer's order is received until the moment the goods are dispatched.
   See also *supply chain.*

GRN (Goods Received Note) Document, or computer entry, raised to indicate the receipt of goods, giving details of quantity, description and supplier. It would normally also indicate the order against which the delivery was booked.

Groupage Consolidation of several consignments into a container, or by road onto a trailer, or by air as one consignment under the sponsorship of one agent.
   See also *consolidation.*

HAZCHEM (Hazardous Chemicals) Regulations covering the carriage of hazardous chemicals by road.
   See *TREMCARDS,* and also Chapter 2.

HMSO Her Majesty's Stationery Office (UK only).

ICAO Instructions International Civil Aviation Organisation Technical Instructions covering the carriage of dangerous goods by air.
   See Chapter 2.

ICC International Chamber of Commerce.

IMDG (International Maritime Dangerous Goods Code) Code covering the movement of dangerous goods by sea.
   See Chapter 2.

Imprest stock Stock dedicated to a specific customer and quite often stored on the customer's premises. It remains the property of the supplier until drawn off by the customer. At that point the customer will be invoiced.

It differs from *consignment stock* in that, as drawings are made, the stock is replenished to the agreed level.

INCOTERMS Published by the International Chamber of Commerce in English and French. Although not mandatory they set out the generally accepted definitions of the standard shipping terms used in trade. They clearly set out the responsibilities of buyer and seller.

See Chapter 7.

ISO (International Standards Organisation) Geneva-based organisation responsible for producing internationally accepted standards. While not mandatory they are increasingly accepted, particularly in Europe which is responsible for more than 60 per cent of published standards. They often duplicate national standards.

IT (Information Technology) The application of hardware (machinery) and software (systems and techniques) to methods of processing and presenting data into a meaningful form which helps reduce uncertainty and is of real perceived value in current or future decisions.

JIT (Just in Time) An inventory control philosophy whose goal is to maintain just enough material in just the right place at just the right time to make just the right amount of product.

See White, Lee (1985) 'What is it and how does it affect DP', Computer World, June 1985.

Lead time The time taken to meet a requirement. It is normally measured from the time when the need was identified to the time the need is fully met.

Actual delivery time is a component part of lead time, but only measures transportation and does not include all the activities involved in documentation, order processing, etc.

Marketing mix Product, pricing, promotion, distribution.

MFA (Multi-Fibre Arrangement) A series of mainly bilateral agreements to regulate trade in textiles between developing countries and traditional western producers.

MFN (Most Favoured Nation) 'Each contracting party shall accord to the commerce of the other contracting parties treatment no less favourable than that provided for in the Schedule Annexed to this Agreement': Article II.1a, GATT.

Mission statement Concise and unambiguous statement of objectives.

MRP1 (Materials Requirements Planning) A set of logically related procedures, decision rules and records designed to translate a master production schedule into time-phased net requirements.

MRP2 (Manufacturing Resource Planning) A closed loop system which acts as a model of the organisation, making it possible to evaluate the effects of changes in the various inputs coming into the business. It is normally considered to encompass:

- master production scheduling;
- materials requirements planning (MRP1);
- production system planning;
- production capacity planning and control;
- production scheduling.

NAFTA (North American Free Trade Area) Currently (1995) USA, Mexico, Canada.

OCR (Optical Character Recognition) Equipment which can 'read' documents and feed the information into a computer system. Sometimes the numbers or letters (as with bank cheques) have to be printed in a stylised manner.

OECD (Organisation for Economic Cooperation and Development) Consisting of the richer nations of the world, acts as a forum for expanding trade, maintaining financial stability and contributing to the economic expansion of the Third World.

OPEC (Organisation of Petroleum Exporting Countries) Currently (1995) consists of Algeria, Ecuador, Gabon, Indonesia, Iran, Iraq, Kuwait, Libya, Nigeria, Qatar, Saudi Arabia, United Arab Emirates, Venezuela. Aims to maximise revenues of producer states. Very powerful in the late 1970s.

Outsourcing Using a third party to perform work which has normally been carried out by the organisation itself.

Palletisation Utilisation of a platform device for moving and storing goods. Pallets can be two-way entry or four-way entry.

Pareto analysis The application to business problems of Pareto's law. Pareto observed that the minority of the population owned the majority of the wealth of his country. The application of this process of analysis helps the manager to separate the essential few from the trivial many.

Also known as ABC analysis and the 80/20 rule (80 per cent of deliveries made to 20 per cent of the customers).

Partnership (sourcing) A continuous relationship, based on mutual trust and mutual benefits, between two companies.

Also known as co-maker (Europe) or co-vendor (USA).

Performance Ratio of actual output to standard (normally as set in the operating budget).

Productivity Ratio of real output to real input.

Profit centre An activity which employs capital, generates income, sets prices and adds value. It can also, of course, incur losses.

RDT (Radio Data Terminal)
Truck-mounted or hand-held terminal which facilitates the transmission of on-line, real-time information to and from the host computer.

REC Regional electricity company (UK only).

Remains See *back order.*

RID (Réglement International Dangeroux) International agreement covering international carriage of dangerous goods by rail.

See Chapter 2.

SAD (Single Administrative Document) A multi-purpose eight-part document set designed to cover all forms required to make an import or export entry. Normally split into its various copies for use. Known officially in the UK as Customs Form C88.

Service level Percentage of orders (or order lines) totally met from stock without creating a back order.

SITPRO (Simpler Trade Procedures Board) UK government agency established in 1970 whose role is to guide, stimulate and assist the rationalisation of international trade procedures and the documentation and information flows associated with them.

SPIN Southampton Port Information Service. See Chapter 1.

Sub-optimisation Whole less than the sum of the parts.

SUMED Suez–Mediterranean Pipeline. See Chapter 1.

Supply chain The total movement of goods, from the initial supplier through the organisation and on to the end customer. See also *goods flow*.

Conceptually the supply chain falls into three parts:

(a) inbound logistics – from the initial supplier to the organisation;
(b) internal logistics – movement within the organisation;
(c) outbound logistics – from the organisation to the end customer.

SWOT analysis Analysing company or situation by:

- Strengths
                          } Internal;
- Weaknesses

- Opportunities
                          } External.
- Threats

See Chapter 4.

Synergy Whole greater than the sum of the parts.

TEU (Twenty foot Equivalent Unit) Unit of measure used for calculating the capacity of container ships. See Chapter 2.

Third party The outside party (ie not part of the company) to a transaction or agreement.

TIR (Transport International Routier) An international convention under which a TIR approved vehicle meets the requirement that it is possible to seal it securely.

A TIR vehicle can therefore be sealed by customs authorities at the point of departure and can then cross borders without detailed inspection of the contents. TIR carnets can be obtained for such vehicles delivering loads outside the EU, or bringing in loads from outside the EU.

Trade-off Situation where an increased cost in one area is more than matched by a cost reduction in another.

TREMCARD (Transport Emergency Card) Written information covering the chemical identity of the material carried, action to be taken in an emergency and appropriate first-aid procedures. It should also give a contact telephone number for advice. This must be carried in the cab of the vehicle carrying the product, and must be printed in the language of each of the countries the vehicle will pass through.

See also *HAZCHEM*.

Unitisation Combining a number of packages into one unit by strapping, banding, shrink-wrapping or otherwise attaching them together.

VAT (Value Added Tax) Known in France as TVA this tax, which is calculated on a percentage basis, is applicable to a wide range of goods and services. Normally payable on a *destination* basis, ie by the buyer.

VDU (Visual Display Unit) A terminal which can receive or display data on a screen.

WTO World Trade Organisation – successor to GATT (1995).

APPENDIX I: ALTERNATIVE TRANSPORT MODES: ADVANTAGES AND DISADVANTAGES

AIR TRANSPORT

Advantages

- *Transit.* Speedy between air terminals. Useful for lightweight overseas trade, emergencies or where goods have short lives, eg flowers, newspapers.
- *Packing.* Normally only light coverage is necessary as greater care is taken of goods.
- *Insurance.* Less risk and normally cheaper than other forms of freight insurance providing goods are of relatively low weight.
- *Security.* Good.

Disadvantages

- *Transit.* The shorter the journey terminal to terminal, the proportionally greater the time spent getting to and from the airport.
- *Packing.* Although containers have been devised for use in cargo carrying aircraft there is still a limitation in size and weight.
- *Weather.* Can be affected by adverse weather conditions.
- *Costs.* Can be high in relation to other forms of transit.
- *Infrastructure.* Needs airport facilities.

RAIL TRANSPORT

Advantages

- *Loads.* Almost any type of commodity can be moved by rail often in specially assembled trains.
- *Costs.* Charges are negotiable and can be very low per tonne/mile for bulk, particularly if there is a regular movement.
- *Warehousing.* Outside dedicated distribution companies the railways have major warehousing facilities.
- *Private sidings.* Private sidings can be connected to the public network to permit discharge when convenient.

Disadvantages

- *Transit.* Deliveries for specific times and dates cannot be guaranteed for general traffic. The further the customer is from the main line, the greater the risk of delay due to shunting, transshipment, etc.
- *Packing.* The nature of the railway operation means that goods can be damaged if not adequately packed. Packaging normally has to be stronger than that used for other transport media.
- *Deterioration or damage.* Can be caused by contamination from other products carried in the same wagon.
- *Infrastructure.* Needs network or track to operate and terminals for loading/unloading.

ROAD TRANSPORT

Advantages

- *Flexibility.* Goods can be moved between any number of points without the need for specially built terminals.
- *Delivery.* Normally prompt and traceable, and can be made without transshipping in many cases.
- *Costs.* Comparative and negotiable – many private operators.

Disadvantages

- *Environmental.* Legislation against pollution and congestion.

- *Road condition.* Weather, repairs (particularly on motorways).
- *Costs.* Can be expensive for a small parcel if there is no other consignment.

WATER (SEA AND INLAND WATERWAYS)

Advantages

- *Costs.* Cheapest way of moving bulk long distances.

Disadvantages

- *Packing.* Must be strong to cope with handling and environment. (NB: The situation has greatly improved with containerisation.)
- *Transit.* Very slow method of delivery.
- *Weather.* Can affect delivery, and in some cases stop it altogether (eg ice in sub-polar regions).
- *Infrastructure.* Port and docking facilities required.

APPENDIX 2: STANDARD CONTAINER SIZES

ISO SIZES

20 ft container

- Exterior dimensions: 20 ft (6.1 m) × 8 ft (2.4 m) × 8 ft 6 in (2.6 m)
- Interior dimensions: 5890 mm × 2345 mm × 2400 mm
- Door dimensions: 2335 mm × 2290 mm
- Average cubic capacity: 33.3 m³
- Tare weight: 1800/2500 kg depending on construction.

40 ft container

- Exterior dimensions: 40 ft (12.2 m) × 8 ft (2.4 m) × 8 ft 6 in (2.6 m)
- Interior dimensions: 12,015 mm × 2345 mm × 2362 mm
- Average cubic capacity: 66.9 m³
- Tare weight: varies between 3700 and 4380 kg depending on construction.

Containers are generally built to the above ISO Standards but there are still some 35 ft and 30 ft containers in service. Although 8 ft 6 in has been adopted as the definitive standard for height, many containers built to the original 8 ft dimension are also still being used.

CONTAINER TYPES

Containers can be obtained in many types. The most common are:

- end loading   – hard top;
- end and top loading   – canvas/open top;

- end, side and top loading – half height side walls;
- end, side and top loading – canvas cover (TIR);
- end loading   – insulated and refrigerated.

APPENDIX 3: ROUTEING CHECKLIST

Vehicle scheduling and routeing: checklist of vital points

1. *Type of system*
   (a) Do you operate a fixed day or fixed interval system?
   (b) Do you operate a fixed route system? If so, are you confident that your demand pattern is sufficiently stable to merit this type of system?
   (c) What is the number of days which elapse between receiving the order and delivery of the goods?
   (d) Does it allow you sufficient flexibility for efficient load planning?
   (e) Do delivery calls have to be made in reverse order of loading? Or has the driver access to each part of his load?

2. *Standards of operation*
   (a) Have you made an objective assessment of the work content of the different aspects of a driver's task?
       (i) Driving at standard speed set for travel along motorways, trunk roads, A and B class roads, unclassified roads, urban and city routes?
       (ii) Calling at customers?
       (iii) Unloading at customers?
       (iv) Collecting of empties or returns?
       (v) Depot work at start and finish of each journey?
   (b) What is the standard working day or week?
   (c) Can you extend this where necessary?

3. *Routeing*
   (a) What is your primary objective and is it compatible with customer satisfaction?

      (i)   To maximise a driver's work content?

      (ii) To maximise a vehicle capacity utilisation?

      (iii) To minimise mileage travelled?

      (iv) To minimise number of vehicles?

(b) Do you maximise initially on the use of the most expensive resource?

(c) Is this the driver or vehicle?

(d) Can you group demand points together to facilitate the routeing process?

(e) If so, do you use some type of grid system for this purpose?

(f) In building up your routes, do you separate the fixed work content, such as unloading or calling at customers, from the variable element, such as distance travelled?

(g) Do you follow fixed patterns in building up your own routes or explore at each stage the different options open?

(h) How do you accommodate delivery restrictions?

(i) Can your planned routeing be completed within the legal requirements relating to drivers' hours?

(j) When did you last check the mechanism of your current routeing system?

4. *Scheduling*

(a) Do your vehicles undertake more than one journey per day?

(b) If so, how do you ensure that the best selection of journeys is made for each vehicle?

(c) Do all vehicles leave together at the beginning of the day or is it necessary to have a staggered start?

(d) Is your operation affected by rush hour congestion?

(e) Is it better to avoid certain periods of the day when leaving or returning to depot?

(f) What delivery time restrictions do you have to observe?

(g) Where these are difficult to fit have you asked your customer to be more flexible?

(h) Do you use a booking system for selecting delivery calls?

5. *Type of vehicle*

(a) What is the capacity constraint – is this a weight or volume factor?

(b) Do you operate the correct size vehicle for your task, eg would a larger vehicle lead to a more efficient operation?

(c) Why?

(d) How does this compare with the vehicles you have?

(e) Can your vehicles be loaded/unloaded by mechanical means, eg by fork lift truck?

6. *Contingencies*

(a) Do you know which contingencies delay your driver?

(b) Do you record and analyse these delays?

(c) What action do you take concerning major and repetitive delays?

(d) Is queuing a problem?

(e) Have you assessed the effect of queuing upon your delivery schedules?

(f) Have you approached your customers with factual evidence?

(g) Have you built into your schedule allowances for contingencies commonly met?

7. *Control*

(a) How do you measure performance? Do you assess:
  (i)   driver performance?
  (ii) driver utilisation?
  (iii) vehicle utilisation?
  (iv) delay time?
  (v)   time spent in the depot?

(b) Do you compare actual performance against what you might have achieved?

(c) What action do you take when performance falls below plan?

8. *Responsibility*

(a) Who has responsibility for checking vehicle schedules?

(b) Who authorises these schedules?

(c) Who has the authority to override the schedule or make special deliveries?

(d) Who takes responsibility for the cost of special deliveries?

Reproduced from *The Distribution Study Guide* (Chartered Institute of Purchasing and Supply, 1995).

APPENDIX 4: EXAMPLES OF COMPUTERISED CONTROL REPORTS

The following reports are taken from the booklet *System Overview,* published by RTSI Ltd, the UK subsidiary of ROADSHOW International Inc, producers of the ROADSHOW computer-based routing system.

ROUTE SHEET

```
ROUTE NAME: ROUTE005  DATE: 05/04/94  CLASS: 1  SET: *        PAGE 001 05/04/94
                                                              NEWDC    07:09:34
                               ROADSHOW

VEHICLE: REFRIGERATED VAN

DRIVER:  LAKE, BILL                   EMPLOYEE ID:   12

DEPOT:   FALLS CHURCH DEPOT               (DEPOT1  )     LEAVE:  08:49  _____
                                                         ODOM:          _____


GO   SOUTHWEST             0.50 MILES
TO   WASHINGTON ST & BROAD ST                                         WASH-BRO
GO   NORTHWEST (RIGHT)     4.35 MILES
TO   LEESBURG PIKE & MALL ROAD, VIENNA, VA                            LEE-MALL
GO   NORTHEAST (RIGHT)     0.45 MILES

     ..........................................................................

STOP 01: LE MISTRAL                   (MISTRAL  A  )  ARRIVE: 09:00  _____
         TYSONS CORNER SHOPPING CT                    LEAVE:  09:34  _____
         MCLEAN           VA 20012                    ODOM:          _____
         703-555-9800                                 RETURNS:       _____
   >>>>> NOTE: UNLOAD AT DOCK #2

         CUST: LE MISTRAL               ID: 1214000079-0001    MISTRAL
               CONTACT: 703-555-9800        JUDY
   >>>>> NOTE: COD ONLY

               ORDER NO.   TYPE    SIZE   UNIT  COMMODITY        OPEN TIME
               002AHD94    DLVR    68.00  LBS.  PRODUCE          09:00-11:00


GO   SOUTH                 0.05 MILES

     ..........................................................................

STOP 02: WOODIES RESTAURANT           (WOODIES  B  )  ARRIVE: 09:36  _____
         TYSONS CORNER SHOPPING CT                    LEAVE:  10:00  _____
         MCLEAN           VA 20012                    ODOM:          _____
         703-555-1200                                 RETURNS:       _____
   >>>>> NOTE: UNLOAD ON NORTHEAST SIDE

         CUST: WOODIES RESTAURANT       ID: 123400038 -0001    WOODIES
               CONTACT: 703-555-1200        RALPH

               ORDER NO.   TYPE    SIZE   UNIT  COMMODITY        OPEN TIME
               900FE687    DLVR    10.00  CASES MILK            09:00-14:00
```

PERFORMANCE REPORT

VEHICLE: STRAIGHT TRUCK

DRIVER: SMITH, BILL

#	NAME	*** DRIVE TIME ***				*** DELIV TIME ***				****** DISTANCE ******			
		ACT MIN	EXP MIN	DIF MIN	%DIF	ACT MIN	EXP MIN	DIF MIN	%DIF	ACT MIL	EXP MIL	DIF MIL	%DIF
1	JAKES	13	12	1	8	40	37	3	8	6.0	6.0	0	0
2	FARRELLS	15	18	-3	-17	18	18	0	0	6.0	5.5	.5	9
3	CRESTAR	22	24	-2	-8	26	15	11	73	9.7	10.5	-.8	-8
4	ABBYS	25	24	1	4	28	32	-4	-13	5.3	5.3	0	0
5	BISTRO	8	9	-1	-11	10	11	-1	-9	3.0	2.8	.2	7
6	COWLEYS	18	14	4	29	15	16	-1	-6	4.5	3.5	1.0	29
7	BILLIARD	30	28	2	7	5	5	0	0	13.3	13.4	-.1	-1
8	MADHATTER	7	8	-1	-13	35	30	5	17	2.8	2.8	0	0
9	ESTELLES	3	3	0	0	7	8	-1	-13	.7	.7	0	0
10	NATIONS	8	7	1	14	8	10	-2	-20	2.6	2.4	.2	8
11	CAPITAL	34	29	5	17	36	40	-4	-10	16.0	16.1	-.1	-1
12	BAXTERS	15	17	-2	-12	24	23	1	4	8.4	8.2	.2	2
13	FAIRFAX	6	6	0	0	14	11	3	27	2.0	2.0	0	0
14	PEACHES	32	30	2	7	19	17	2	12	14.6	14.9	-.3	-2
	TOTALS	236	229	7	3	285	273	12	4	94.9	94.1	.8	1

TABULAR SUMMARY

```
SUMMARY TABLE          DATE: 05/04/94  CLASS: 1  SET: *        PAGE 001 05/04/94
                                                                       17:31:13
                            ROADSHOW
```

ROUTE/ DISP.	STPS/ UNQ	MILES	DRIVE TIME	TOTAL TIME	LOAD SIZE	----- VEHICLE -----	%FULL	%SUB1	%SUB2	COST/ SOFT	DEP
ROUTE001 05:30	15 14	82	3:28	8:27	4346 lbs 417 cft 1166 cas 4 pal	A 83	0 0	0 0	225 0	1
ROUTE002 06:00	11 9	94	3:22	7:51	5500 lbs 329 cft 97 cas 10 pal	A 75	0 0	0 0	210 0	1
ROUTE003 06:30	10 10	39	2:19	8:01	4856 lbs 622 cft 256 cas 4 pal	A 79	0 0	0 0	127 0	1
ROUTE004 07:00	11 11	69	2:01	8:25	2312 lbs 1018 cft 20 cas	B 92	50 0	0 0	141 0	1
ROUTE005 07:15	15 13	60	1:56	7:26	5612 lbs 325 cft 80 cas 12 pal	A 89	0 0	0 0	155 0	1
ROUTE006 07:30	13 13	80	3:40	7:24	2756 lbs 295 cft 11 cas 18 pal	E 78	0 0	0 0	183 0	1
ROUTE007 07:45	10 8	44	3:32	8:33	2034 lbs 468 cft 262 cas 8 pal	C 81	92 0	30 0	100 0	1
ROUTE008 08:00	7 7	31	2:09	7:53	2791 lbs 196 cft 42 cas 15 pal	D 68	0 0	0 0	96 0	1
TOTAL:	92 85	499	22:27	64:00	30207 lbs 3670 cft 11734 cas 71 pal				1237 0	
AVERAGE:	12 11	62	3:1							

```
DEPOTS:
  1 DEPOT
```

DISPATCH LOG

```
DISPATCHER LOG          DATE: 05/04/94  CLASS: 1  SET:        PAGE 001 05/04/94
                                                                     17:35:57
                            ROADSHOW

ROUTE: ROUTE003

VEHICLE: 16-FT TRAILER
```

#	STOP	OPEN HOURS	LBS.	CFT.	ARRIVE	LEAVE 06:30	PHONE
	DEPOT						
A	ROYS	05:30-10:30	2140.00	328.00	06:45	08:12	301-938-2700
		CUSTOMER ROYS PLACE		CONTACT CHRIS SANDERS		4582109	
B	4H	06:00-14:00	1800.00	308.00	08:48	10:27	301-988-2429
		CUSTOMER NATIONAL 4-H COUNCIL		CONTACT BILL DOWNS		4560104 -	
C	FALLS	08:00-14:00	1476.00	222.00	10:55	13:20	301-981-7100
		CUSTOMER RIVER FALLS CAFE		CONTACT MS. LINZE		4520123	
	DEPOT					15:10	

```
ROUTE 003 TOTALS:
          3 STOPS (  3)       $174.00 ROUTE COST     67.20 MILES
          3 ORDERS            $ 90.00 LABOR COST      8:40 LABOR HH:MM
          3 CUSTOMERS         $ 84.00 VEHICLE COST    3:09 DRIVE HH:MM

     680.00 CASES             5416.00 LBS.          858.00 CFT.

GRAND TOTALS:
          1 ROUTE
          3 STOPS (  3)       $174.00 ROUTE COST     67.20 MILES
          3 ORDERS            $ 90.00 LABOR COST      8:40 LABOR HH:MM
          3 CUSTOMERS         $ 84.00 VEHICLE COST    3:09 DRIVE HH:MM

     680.00 CASES             5416.00 LBS.          858.00 CFT.
```

PROFITABILITY REPORT

PROFITABILITY		DATE: 05/05/94	CLASS: 1	SET:		PAGE 001	05/05/94
			ROADSHOW			NEWDC	07:56:33

ROUTE	REVENUE	VEHICLE	-----COSTS----- STRAIGHT	OVERTIME	TOTAL	NET
ROUTE01 -	4908.00	89.02	122.96	8.68	220.66	4687.34
8 STOPS	613.50	11.13	15.37	1.09	27.58	585.92
818 CASE	6.00	0.11	0.15	0.01	0.27	05.73
ROUTE02	3468.96	47.68	105.60	0.00	153.28	3315.68
11 STOPS	315.36	4.33	9.60	0.00	13.93	301.43
432 CASE	8.03	0.11	0.24	0.00	0.35	7.68
ROUTE03	3927.00	94.87	106.30	0.35	201.52	3725.48
15 STOPS	261.80	6.32	7.09	0.02	13.43	248.37
374 CASE	10.50	0.25	0.28	0.00	0.54	9.96
ROUTE04	12046.32	125.93	126.01	10.20	262.14	11784.18
9 STOPS	1338.48	13.99	14.00	1.13	29.13	1309.35
1716 CASE	7.02	0.07	0.07	0.01	0.15	6.87
ROUTE05	5807.52	57.50	105.60	0.00	163.10	5644.42
12 STOPS	483.96	4.79	8.80	0.00	13.59	470.37
654 CASE	8.88	0.09	0.16	0.00	0.25	8.63
ROUTE06	6748.80	163.62	117.56	5.98	287.16	6461.64
15 STOPS	449.92	10.91	7.84	0.40	19.14	430.78
608 CASE	11.10	0.27	0.19	0.01	0.47	10.63
ROUTE07	6554.88	109.56	126.72	10.56	246.84	6308.04
5 STOPS	409.68	6.85	7.92	0.66	15.43	394.75
51 CASE	11.52	0.19	0.22	0.02	0.43	11.09
ROUTE08	5577.76	22.12	105.60	0.00	127.72	5450.04
16 STOPS	348.61	1.38	6.60	0.00	7.98	340.63
491 CASE	11.36	0.05	0.22	0.00	0.26	11.10
ROUTE09	4417.92	54.93	105.60	0.00	160.53	4257.39
13 STOPS	339.84	4.23	8.12	0.00	12.35	327.49
472 CASE	9.36	0.12	0.22	0.00	0.34	9.02
TOTAL	53457.16	765.23	1021.95	35.77	1822.95	51633.91
9 ROUTES	5937.68	85.03	113.55	3.97	202.55	5737.10
115 STOPS	464.84	6.65	8.89	0.31	15.85	448.99
6134 CASE	8.71	0.12	0.17	0.01	0.30	8.42

CUSTOMER ARRIVAL TIMES

ARRIVAL TIME SUMMARY		DATE: 05/04/94	CLASS: 1	SET: *		PAGE 001	05/04/94
			ROADSHOW				17:35:57

CUSTOMER ID			NAME	STOP	ROUTE	STP #	DAY/ TRIP	ARRIV LEAVE
ABBYS	2323455	-0001	ABBY'S CAFE	AIRRIGHT	ROUTE003	4	1	09:00-09:22
ALEXANDR	0607701	-	ALEXANDRIA HOSP	ALEXANDR	ROUTE004	9	1	11:15-12:00
ALPINE	1234000	-0002	ALPINE RESTAUR	AIRRIGHT	ROUTE005	12	1	10:50-11:14
AMERICAN	07L2001	-	AMERICAN UNIVE	AMERICAN	ROUTE003	10	1	12:54-13:10
ANDREE	1007369	-	ANDREE RESTAU	ANDREE	ROUTE004	4	1	08:00-08:16
BANNER	60C0722	-	BANNER SPORT B	BANNER	ROUTE006	3	1	08:25-08:42
BARKLEYS	60C0723	-	BARKLEY'S BAR	BARKLEYS	ROUTE002	5	1	07:35-07:42
BAXTERS	60C0642	-	BAXTER'S LODGE	BAXTERS	ROUTE006	9	1	10:07-10:17
BEACH	6015781	-	BEACH HOUSE	BEACH	ROUTE005	8	1	09:48-09:56
BIDDLE	9966109	-	BIDDLE INN	BIDDLE	ROUTE005	2	1	07:55-08:17
BILLIARD	60C1110	-	BILLIARD HOUSE	BILLIARD	ROUTE002	8	1	08:45-08:53
BILLS	60C1653	-	BILL'S DELI	BILLS	ROUTE006	4	1	08:51-08:58
BINDER	6012218	-	BINDER CAFE	BINDER	ROUTE005	3	1	08:32-08:40
BISTRO	60C9526	-	BISTRO ITALIANO	BISTRO	ROUTE004	1	1	07:10-07:19
BLACK	1234000	-0001	BLACK ORCHID	BANKBUIL	ROUTE006	2	1	08:01-08:23
BLAIRS	60C3833	-	BLAIR'S LOUNGE	BLAIRS	ROUTE001	8	1	08:42-08:56
BORDERS	60C8537	-	BORDER'S STORE	BORDERS	ROUTE004	6	1	08:42-09:05

MILES BY STATE

```
MILES BY STATE          DATE: 05/04/94  CLASS: 1  SET: *        PAGE 001 05/04/94
                                                                         17:31:01
                                ROADSHOW

                --------APPROXIMATE MILES DRIVEN BY STATE--------

ROUTE            NC        MD        PA        VA        WV
ROUTE001         0.0     102.9       0.0      24.5       0.0
ROUTE002         0.0       0.0       0.0     290.6       0.0
ROUTE003        29.9       0.0       0.0     512.2       0.0
ROUTE004         0.0      60.8       0.0     122.4       0.0
ROUTE005         0.0      29.1      22.0     186.7      52.0

  TOTALS:       29.9     192.8      22.0    1136.4      52.0
```

APPENDIX 5: WAREHOUSING CHECKLIST OF VITAL POINTS

1. **General points**
   (a) Do you need a warehouse?
       (i) Could your suppliers carry your stocks?
       (ii) Would it be economical to pay someone else to do your warehousing?
       (iii) Is it possible to meet requirements with temporary warehouses?

   (b) Is the warehouse in the right place?
       (i) What is your current and future distribution network?
       (ii) Where are customers located?
       (iii) What forms of communication, services and transport are required now and in the future?

2. **Warehouse operation**
   (a) Has the situation – buildings and equipment – been studied in detail?
   (b) Are you sure that you know the shortcomings of the present layout?
   (c) Have you determined the basic flow of goods and the activity and space relationships of the various functions in the warehouse?
   (d) Has an 'ideal' layout been planned, regardless of cost or other restrictions, to make sure that no opportunities have been missed?
   (e) Has the 'ideal' layout been adapted to a realistic layout?
   (f) Have you adequately planned the detail, using work study techniques?
   (g) If you are changing your layout has the changeover been planned to take place at the most suitable time?

(h) Does the layout minimise movement of goods?

(i) Is it flexible – will alterations be relatively easy?

(j) Have you remembered the human relations aspect and let everyone know what you are doing – and why?

(k) Has everyone been consulted and given the opportunity to contribute to the new layout?

(l) Will the operatives be satisfied with all conditions?

3. *Equipment*

(a) What is the size, weight, value and throughput of each merchandise group handled?

(b) Do you know the physical limitations of the warehouse (eg floorloading, ramps, gradients, accessibility)?

(c) Are there any special needs (eg stock rotation, security)?

(d) Have you considered every possible way of moving the goods – and costed each?

(e) Do you have the necessary specialist knowledge – or should external advice be sought?

4. *Personnel*

(a) Are your operatives generally satisfied with working conditions?

(b) Are your wages comparable with similar local warehouses?

(c) Is your labour force stable – or have you a high labour turnover?

(d) Are your communications good – or is there a 'grapevine'?

(e) Are operatives able to air their ideas, feelings and grievances openly?

(f) Is management fair in its response?

(g) Do you expect your operatives to work excessive overtime?

(h) Are workers adequately motivated to work? Do you operate an incentive scheme?

(i) Are workers paid in relation to their responsibilities and effort?

(j) Is the labour force sufficiently flexible to accommodate a fluctuating work load?

(k) Do management, operatives and unions trust and respect each other?

Reproduced from *The Distribution Study Guide* (Chartered Institute of Purchasing and Supply, 1995).

APPENDIX 6: EXPORT/IMPORT DOCUMENTATION

The information given in this appendix is reproduced from the Midland Bank plc publication *Letters of Credit*.

Letter of Credit

Uniform Customs and Practice states that all instructions regarding letters of credit, their issue and any amendment that may be necessary, should be clear and precise. But there is one useful area of flexibility, and that concerns the word *about*. When referring to the amount or the quantity of items or the unit price of the goods, *about* means plus or minus 10%.

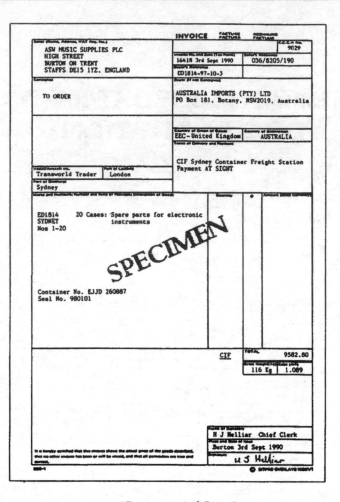

Commercial Invoice

The documents most commonly stipulated for presentation by an exporter under a letter of credit are as follows:

COMMERCIAL INVOICE

The invoice is a claim by the exporter for payment from the importer under the terms of the sales contract. It should include a description of the goods, together with unit prices, if appropriate, amount payable, shipping marks and shipping terms. All these details must also match exactly the information stipulated in the letter of credit. Normally several copies of the invoice are required by the customs authorities overseas. The invoice should also state the price of the goods as agreed by both importer and exporter, using the standard price terms (Incoterms).

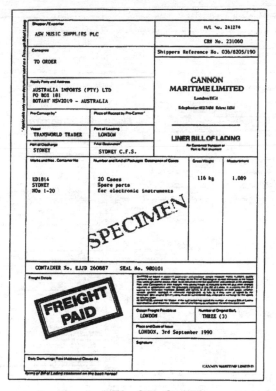

Bill of Lading

BILL OF LADING

This document is the receipt given to the exporter by the shipping company for goods accepted for transport by sea. It conveys title to the goods when in negotiable form. The bill of lading names the shipper and the consignee (importer) or the consignee's agent and it is signed on behalf of the carrier. If it is issued to *order*, it is transferable by the party named as shipper or, if issued to the order of a named party, it is transferable by that party, in both cases by endorsement.

Bills of lading are normally issued in sets of two, three or more originals, any one of which may be used to obtain delivery of the goods. The number of originals in a set is shown on each document. As soon as one original is presented to the carrier at the port of destination in order to obtain release of the goods, the carrier's liability is discharged even if the true owner were to present another original. For complete control over the goods, therefore, it is necessary to possess a full set. Non-negotiable copies, which are unsigned, are not documents of title and are used only for record purposes. Most letters of credit call for full sets to be presented to the bank before the exporter is paid.

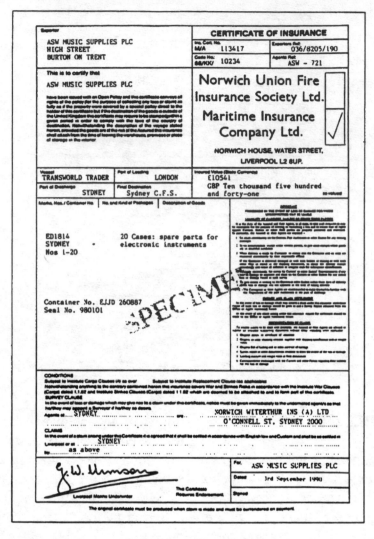

Insurance Certificate

INSURANCE POLICY OR CERTIFICATE

Proof that the goods are covered for risk of damage or loss during transit is often asked for in the letter of credit, which will call for either an insurance policy or an insurance certificate. (However, certificates issued by insurance brokers are not acceptable unless specifically permitted by the credit.)

Regular exporters can arrange to cover all exports over a particular period, thereby avoiding the need to take out a fresh policy with each shipment. In this case individual insurance certificates are issued for each shipment – either by the insurers or by the exporter.

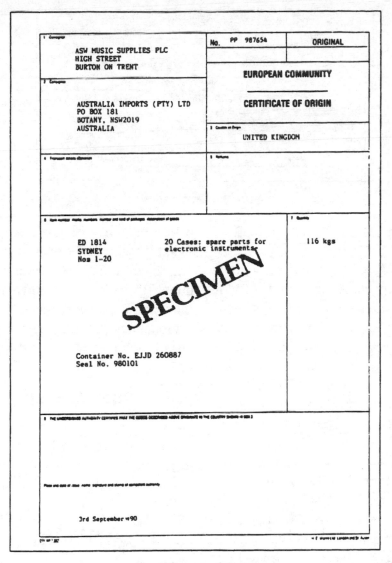

Certificate of Origin

CERTIFICATE OF ORIGIN

Most countries require a certificate which shows evidence of the country of origin of the goods being imported. Letters of credit often stipulate the presentation of this document, which may be issued by the exporter himself or by a chamber of commerce or consular authority, as specified.

Sometimes the credit may call for a special combined certificate of value and origin and invoice. This is completely separate from the commercial invoice.

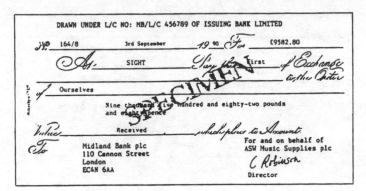

Bill of Exchange

BILLS OF EXCHANGE

A bill of exchange is legally defined as 'an unconditional order in writing, addressed by one person to another, signed by the person giving it, requiring the person to whom it is addressed to pay on demand or at a fixed or determinable future time a sum certain in money to, or to the order of, a specified person or to bearer'.

In the case of a letter of credit transaction, it is drawn up by the exporter (the drawer), and is an order to the importer or the paying bank (the drawee) to pay a specified amount of money immediately (a sight bill) or at a future date (a usance bill). The example shown is of a sight bill. In the case of a usance bill, the drawee acknowledges and accepts liability for the exporter's claim for payment by signing an acceptance across it. The wording on the bill of exchange must match exactly the terms of the credit.

A single bill of exchange (called a *sola* bill) may be presented, provided that the credit does not stipulate that bills are required in duplicate. Bill of exchange forms may normally be purchased from stationers, or they may even be produced on a company's own headed notepaper.

AIR WAYBILL

Goods which are transported by air require a waybill to act as receipt for dispatch, detailing all the information about the flight and destination.

COMBINED TRANSPORT DOCUMENT

When goods are carried by more than one method of transport (particularly containers), a combined transport or through container document is often used.

FORWARDING AGENT'S CERTIFICATE OF RECEIPT

A forwarder uses this as evidence of receipt and/or dispatch of goods.

APPENDIX 7: FREIGHT FORWARDERS

The basic role of the freight forwarder (or forwarding agent) is to provide some or all of the following services:

- To provide advice on packing, routeing, documentation and insurance from an up-to-date knowledge of rates, regulations, conditions and availability.
- To obtain quotations for these services from competing sources.
- To perform the role of consolidation or groupage agent.
- To clear goods through customs at both shipping points (entry and exit).
- To act as an information source in the trade or community.

The British International Freight Association (0181-844 2266) publishes a booklet *A Brief Introduction to Freight Forwarding* which gives insight into the services a freight forwarder can provide.

APPENDIX 8: PROCEDURE FOR TRANSPORTING DANGEROUS GOODS

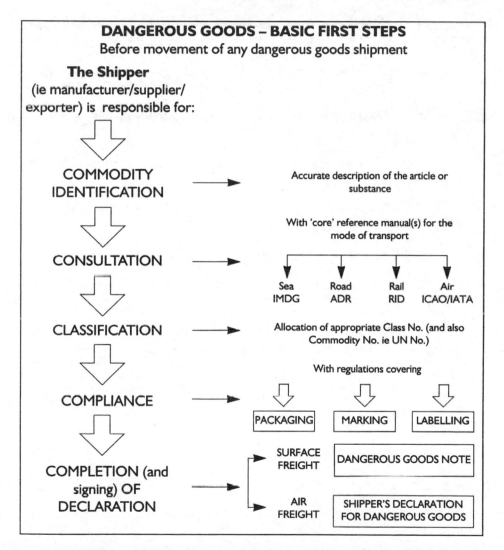

DANGEROUS GOODS – BASIC FIRST STEPS
Before movement of any dangerous goods shipment

The Shipper
(ie manufacturer/supplier/
exporter) is responsible for:

COMMODITY
IDENTIFICATION → Accurate description of the article or substance

CONSULTATION → With 'core' reference manual(s) for the mode of transport

Sea	Road	Rail	Air
IMDG	ADR	RID	ICAO/IATA

CLASSIFICATION → Allocation of appropriate Class No. (and also Commodity No. ie UN No.)

COMPLIANCE → With regulations covering

PACKAGING   MARKING   LABELLING

COMPLETION (and signing) OF DECLARATION →

SURFACE FREIGHT → DANGEROUS GOODS NOTE

AIR FREIGHT → SHIPPER'S DECLARATION FOR DANGEROUS GOODS

Reproduced from Derek Downs, *Understanding the Freight Business*, Micor Freight UK Ltd.

SPECIALIST BIBLIOGRAPHY

Branch, A E (1990) *Elements of Import Practice,* Chapman & Hall, London.

Christopher, M (1990) *The Strategy of Distribution Management,* Heinemann, Oxford.

Cooper, J (ed) (1994) *Logistics and Distribution Planning,* Kogan Page, London.

Coyle, J C, Bardi, E J and Langley Jr, C John (1992) *The Management of Business Logistics,* West Publishing Co, St Paul, Minnesota, USA.

Downs, D E (1992) *Understanding the Freight Business,* Micor Freight UK Ltd, Egham, Surrey.

Dudley, J W (1993) *1993 and Beyond: New Strategies for the Emerging Single Market,* Kogan Page, London.

Fawcett, P, McLeish, R E and Ogden, I D (1992) *Logistics Management,* M&E Handbooks, London.

International Chamber of Commerce (1991) *INCOTERMS 1990,* ICC.

Jessop, D and Morrison, A (1994) *Storage and Supply of Materials,* Pitman, London.

Rushton, A and Oxley, J (1991) *Handbook of Logistics and Distribution Management,* Kogan Page, London.

INDEX